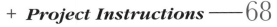

First Edition March 2007
Original Copyright © 2006 Boutique-sha
1-8-3 Hirakawa-cho, Chiyoda-ku, Tokyo 102-0093 Japan

Printed in Japan
ISBN:978-4-88996-214-7

Translator: Yoko Ishiguro

Photographer: Ritsuko Fujita

Project Editors: Yoko Koike
              Kumiko Kozakai

English Editor: Tomomi Ahiko

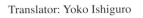

LINEAR PATTERNS

Stitching vertically, horizontally or diagonally... these simple straight lines will be fashioned into attractive sashiko patterns when combined in sequence.

There are only two simple tricks to remember:
1. Shape the corners sharp and clear.
2. Make the stitched line as straight as possible.

Basket Weave
網代 (AJIRO)

This pattern is inspired by thin bamboo or timber strips woven closely in a net-like design. You will find this pattern not only on baskets but also on natural fences. Stitch a pair of narrow rectangles at a time, and avoid stitching into previous seam on the backside, for an evenly tensioned finish.

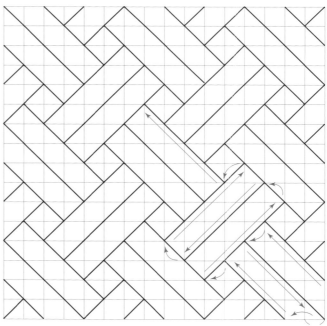

1 square

Hemp Leaf
麻の葉 (ASANOHA)

A representative sashiko pattern composed of six-point star in hexagon. An outer hexagon turns into the vein of a leaf as your eye shifts to any adjacent center circle. Since hemp plants grow straight and quickly, this pattern used to be favored for baby's or children's clothing in the hope of good health.

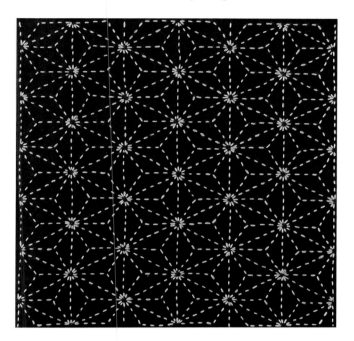

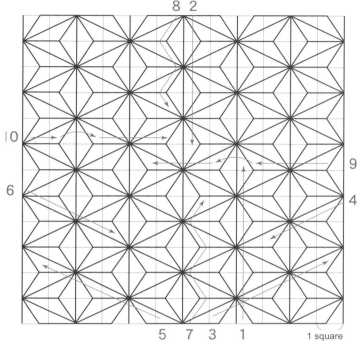

Drawing order

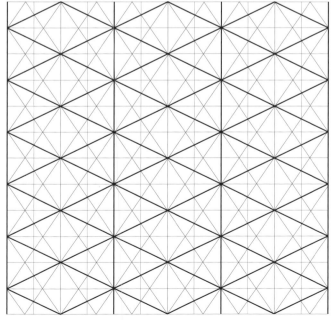

Draw navy-colored vertical lines. Draw navy diagonal lines: 1 square down, 2 squares sideways. Then draw thin red lines diagonally as a guide for leaves : 3 squares vertically, 2 squares sideways.

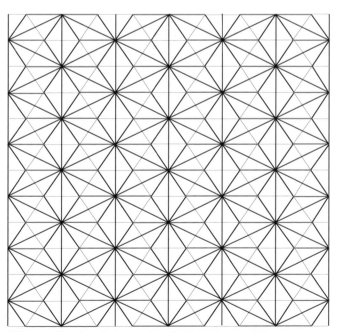

Add navy-colored vertical zigzag lines. Finish by drawing thick red, horizontal lines that clarify the leaf shapes.

Miniaturized Tortoise Shell
霰亀甲 (ARARE-KIKKO)

Tortoise shell pattern (page 9) has created numerous variations including this symmetical hexagon surrounded with downscaled hexagons. *Arare* means hailstones, depicting tiny ice grains scattered over the ground. Begin with stitching vertical lines 1 and 2, and then lateral zigzag lines of 3 to 6 in order. Lastly, stitch remaining verticals of line 7.

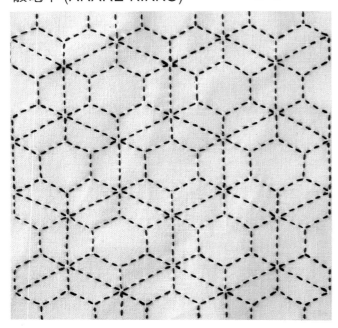

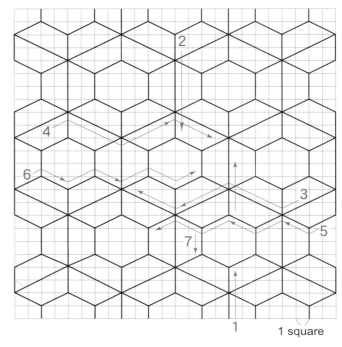

1 square

Well-Frame Check
井桁格子 (IGETA-KOSHI)

The character " 井 " (pronounced as "*e*") stands for well, and *igeta-koshi* is the plaid pattern of this character resembling the framework of well. Stitch a line through, vertically or horizontally, passing the thread on the backside to continue each line without cutting the working thread.

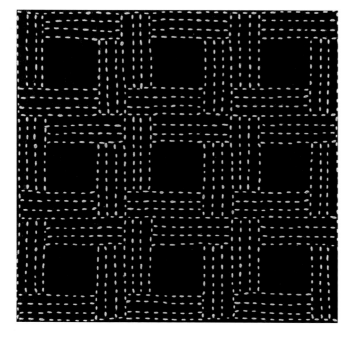

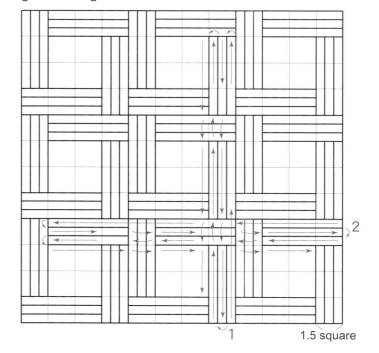

1.5 square

Well Framework
井戸枠 (IDOWAKU)

This design represents a tilted and linked well frames or covers. Stitch one motif at a time: Work outer line 1, and then stitch line 2. Work the corners carefully so that the stitch begins and ends at each pivot point of the motif.

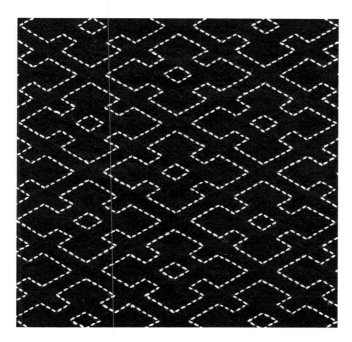

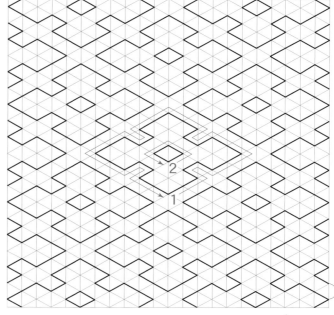

1 square

Angled Seven Treasures
角七宝 (KAKU-SHIPPO)

An angled variation of the Seven Treasures, or Overlapping Circles, on page 39. This version is drawn by dividing a grid into quarters as shown below right. Various expressions will be created by adjusting the proportions of line segments. Work long zigzag line 1, and then work the facing zigzag 2.

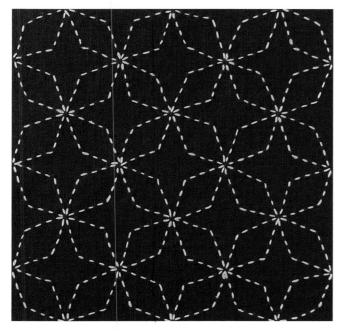

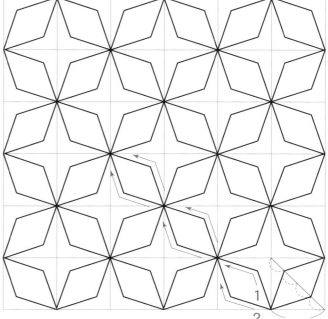

1 square

Linked Squares
角十つなぎ (KAKU-JU-TSUNAGI)

Simple yet amusing design of squares linked to form staircase pattern. Begin with staircase pattern sideways and stitch the small squares. Since a segment has only a few stitches, be sure to create uniform stitches and spaces before forming sharp, right angle corners.

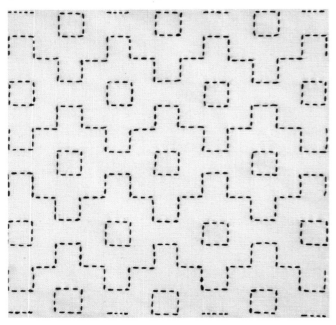

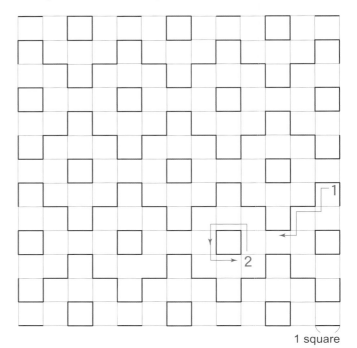

1 square

Storehouse Posts
角寄せ (KAKU-YOSE)

Doubled squares are partially overlaid to symbolize the well-built structure of ancient storehouses. Work on each square, adjusting the stitch length so that you can "stab" into the corner point, which is the key to show your "workmanship".

1 square

Woven Bamboo
篭目 (KAGOME)

Just like a basket made of bamboo strips, a hexagonal open-weave pattern is created with vertical lines intervening with the diamonds. Begin with the vertical stitches, then work the diagonals making sure not to meet the previous stitches as it will ruin the uniformity of little stitches.

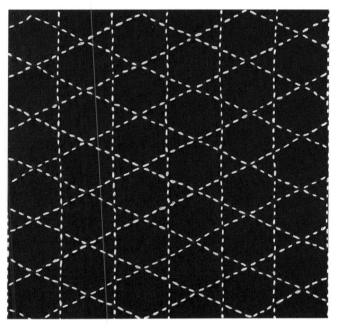

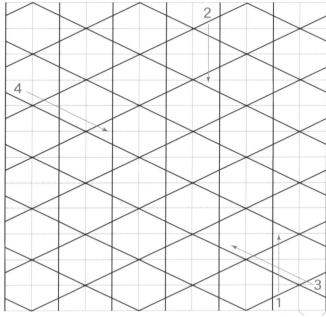

1 square

Floral Pattern
花文 (KAMON)

Cheerful blooming design of linked diamond petals. Be careful when working the center stitches where the five lines meet so that they do not overlap. Begin with straight diagonals 1 and 2, then the outer zigzags 3 and 4. Lastly work the inner zigzags 5 and 6.

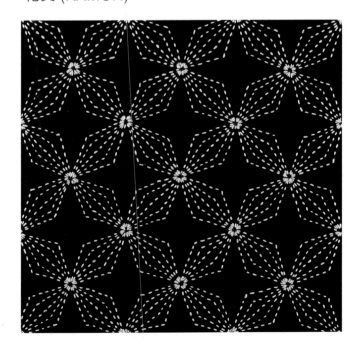

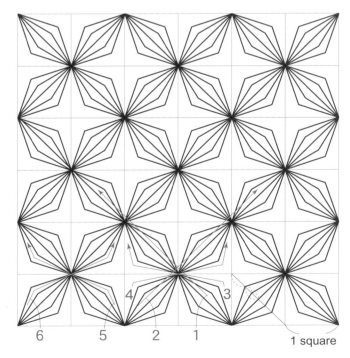

1 square

7

Diagonal Thunderbolt

変わり雷文
(KAWARI-RAIMON)

A variation of Thunderbolt on page 16. This diagonal version has a flowing motion which seems quite different from the original. The seams never intersect each other in this pattern. Be sure to work each stitch as straight as possible for the long running stitches.

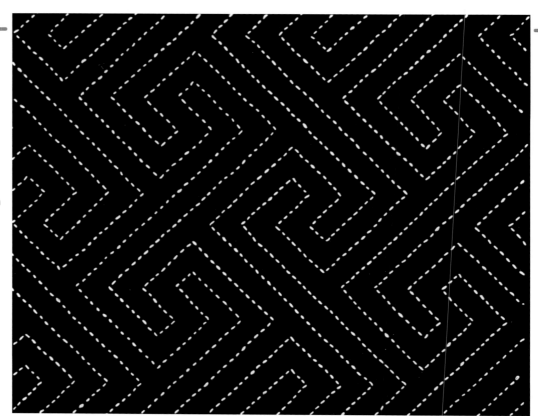

2   1

1 square

Connected Bishamon
変わり毘沙門亀甲
(KAWARI-BISHAMON-KIKKO)

Bishamon is one of the Seven Deities of Good Fortune, and this design was taken from his armor pieces which resembled tortoise shell pattern. Work vertical lines 1 and 2, and then the long diagonals 3 and 4. When stitching line 5, return by passing the thread on the backside to continue the zigzag line.

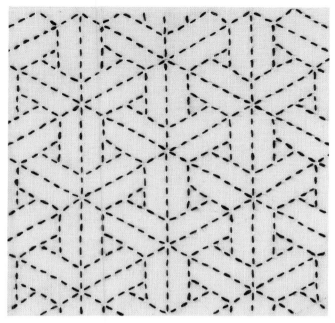

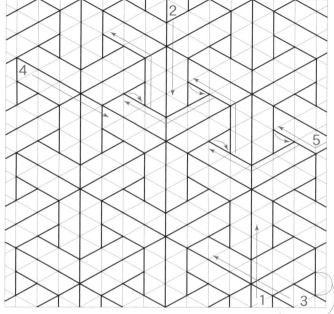

1 square

Tortoise Shell
亀甲 (KIKKO)

A geometric pattern of hexagons brought from west Asian countries where it represented a mysterious existence. Upon its arrival in Japan from China, in the eighth century, it was recognized as the shape of a tortoise shell. Since the tortoise was a symbol of longevity, this pattern has been used in many ways. The design is easy to draw on graph paper. Stitch one pattern each.

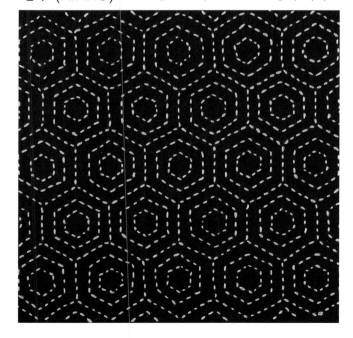

1 square

Glazing Bar Check
組子 (KUMIKO)

Thin strips of wood are interlocked neatly to form a check pattern. The center square is surrounded by four rectangles that are assembled in a chasing pattern. Begin with straight diagonal lines 1 and 2 crossing each other. Then stitch inner sides 3, returning on the backside to continue the four lines. Finish with the outer sides in the same manner.

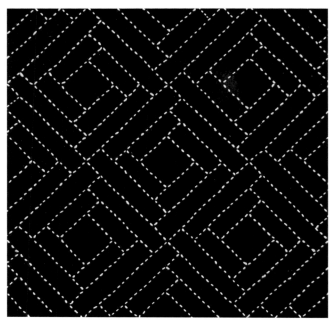

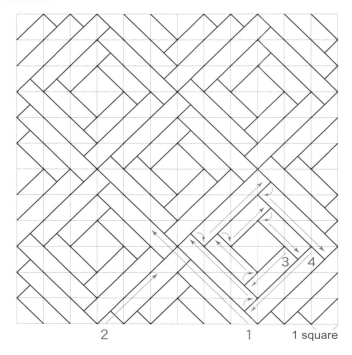

Laticed Diamonds
組菱 (KUMI-HISHI)

This unique pattern is a combination of diamond, cross and rectangle. "*Hishi*" stands for diamond shape nowadays, but originally represented an annual water plant that bears diamond-shaped fruits. As there seems to be no regular method of continuous stitching, plan your own order.

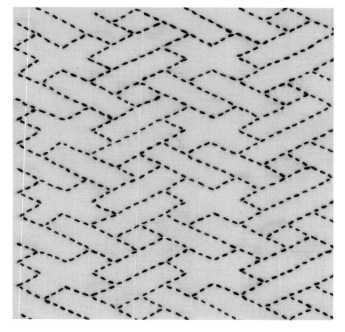

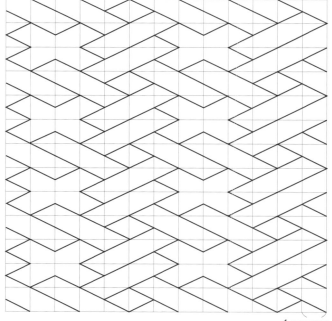

1 square

Linked Checks
格子つなぎ
(KOSHI-TSUNAGI)

Squares seem to be linked diagonally with one another and with a pair of vertical and horizontal lines. Begin with vertical lines 1, then horizontal lines 2. Stitch a square and continue to diagonal line to work another square.

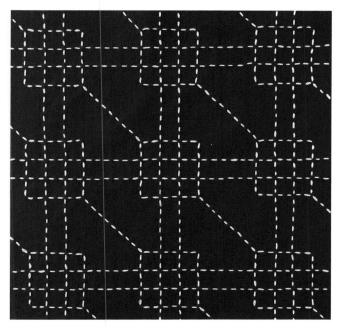

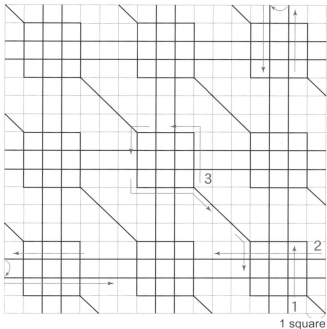

1 square

Tilted Letter "工"
工字崩し
(KOJI-KUZUSI)

The character " 工 " (pronounced as "*ko*") are interlocked each other by placing them closely and diagonally, facing each other. Stitch hooked end and pass the thread on the backside to go on to the adjacent hook. When all the hooks are done, stitch the straight lines.

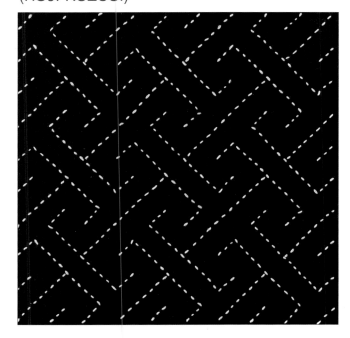

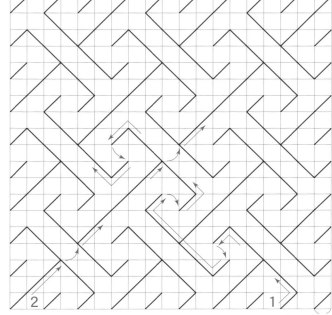

1 square

Key Pattern
紗綾形 (SAYAGATA)

This pattern used to be a must for the white collars of married women's *kimono* on formal occasions. Its motif, swastika, has a long history dating back to Visnu, the Sun God of India. Stitch diagonally through, turning several times until returning to extended, previous diagonal line.

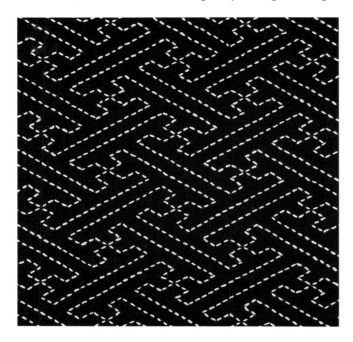

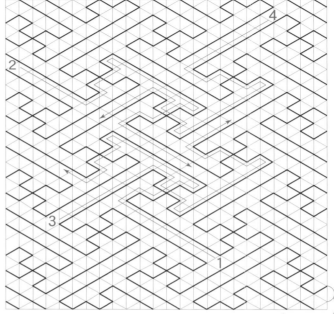

1 square

Squared Key Pattern
紗綾形算崩し (SAYAGATA-SANKUZUSHI)

The " 卍 " (swastikas) are set at right angles in this version, giving a neat geometric impression as "*san*" stands for thin, squared divining blocks. Although the design looks rather complex, you can work in long seams in the same manner as *sayagata*, following the numbers.

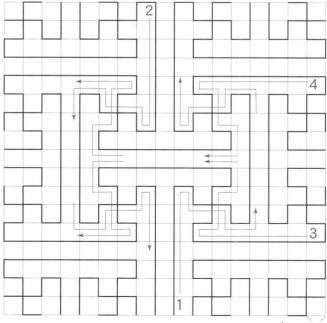

1 square

Triple Diamonds
三重菱つなぎ
(SANJU-HISHI-TSUNAGI)

Inner diamonds are linked with short straight lines to larger diamonds, creating interesting, rounding effect on the corners. First, stitch diagonal lines 1 and 2, then vertical 3. Stitch inner diamonds 4, and finish with horizontal lines 5.

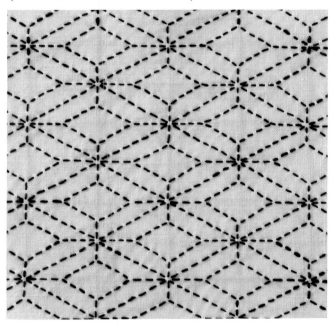

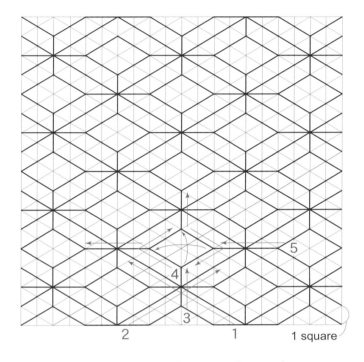

Silk Brocade
蜀紅 (SHOKKO)

Shokko is an old name for Chang Jiang River of China. Its upriver district used to produce good quality silk, and was known for its beautiful brocades including woven flowers or animals in squares and octagons. As it is difficult to stitch in a long seam, work in any order that is convenient for you.

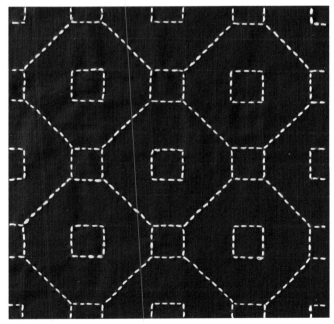

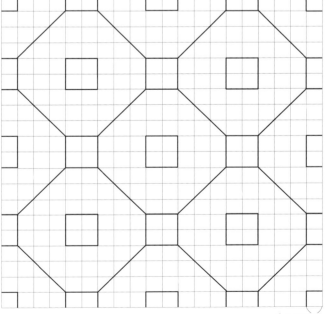

1 square

Cross in Tortoise Shell
十字亀甲 (JUJI-KIKKO)

The hexagon of the *kikko* pattern often encases a flower or animal. In this version, small crosses are stitched inside the tortoise shells, giving a typical hand-stitched impression. Stitch one pattern at a time, a cross-stitch after a hexagon.

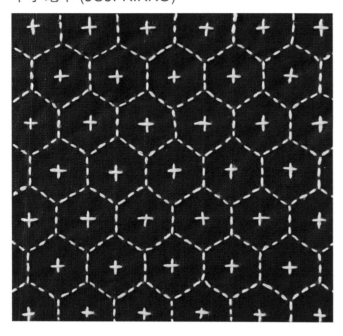

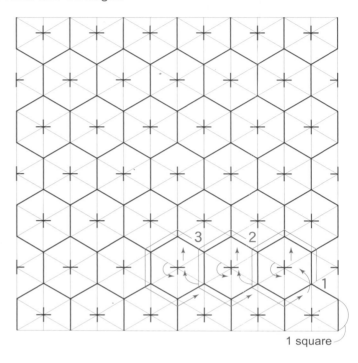

1 square

Linked Cross
十字つなぎ
(JUJI-TSUNAGI)

Fat crosses and hooked crosses can be found next to each other in this design. To stitch, work long, diagonal seams in a step pattern up and down (1 and 2), then sideways (3 and 4) to intersect each other, creating the crosses.

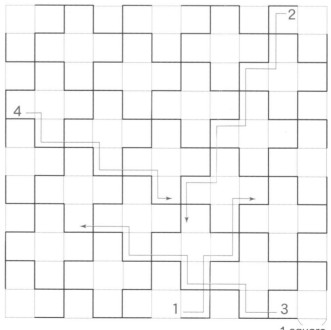

1 square

Tilted Three Nested Boxes
立三枡 (TATE-MIMASU)

Mimasu, or triple measuring boxes, is the *kabuki* crest of the Danjuro Family, one of the most popular troupes of *kabuki* actors. This pattern became very popular in the Edo Period, and people used it in such things as bath towels and everyday *kimono*. Stitch long diagonal lines 1 and 2 to form the outer squares. Then stitch the middle square 3, and the inner square 4.

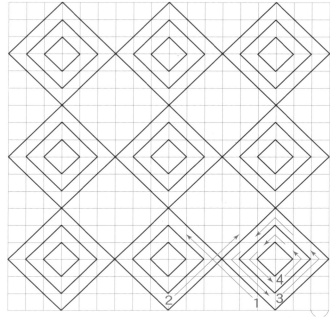

1 square

Stair Steps
段つなぎ (DAN-TSUNAGI)

Simple yet rhythmical pattern worked in one direction. The key to good finish is adjusting your stitch lengths so that you can stab into the pivot points. Also, be careful to make each stitch as straight as possible, which is essential when working in such a simple pattern as this.

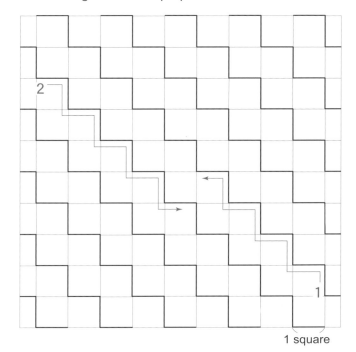

1 square

Mountain Shapes
つづき山形
(TSUZUKI-YAMAGATA)

In Japan, the sign for mountain used to be a letter V upside down since a triangle shape meant a dragon scale. Simple zigzag lines worked vertically and horizontally form this series of high and low mountains. Stitch the pivots as sharp as possible.

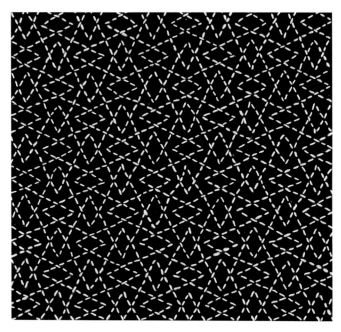

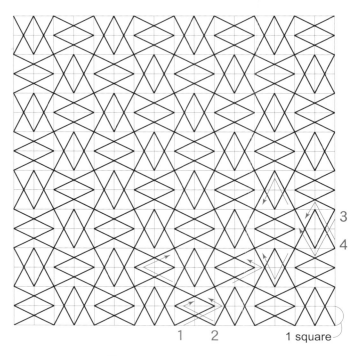

Linked Thunderbolts
つなぎ雷文
(TSUNAGI-RAIMON)

This pattern is derived from the character "雷," resembling the bottom part of it (田). Since thunders bring abundant rain, they were thought to benefit every living thing on earth. Thus this design is also seen in ancient Chinese bronze ware and Greek ceramics or architecture. Stitch a pair at one time, carefully forming sharp corners.

Tortoise Shell Variation
角亀甲 (TSUNO-KIKKO)

Each corner of the tortoise shell is adorned with tiny flower-like stitches. Nevertheless, these corner accents are not stitched separately, but created as you work each hexagon as shown: Begin at line 1, turning back diagonally, thus adding an extra stitch in three directions at the corner. Work next hexagon number 2.

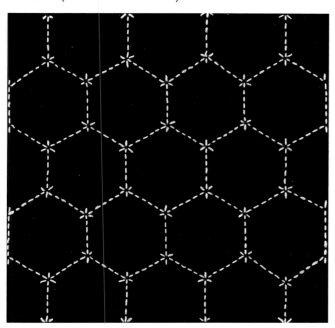

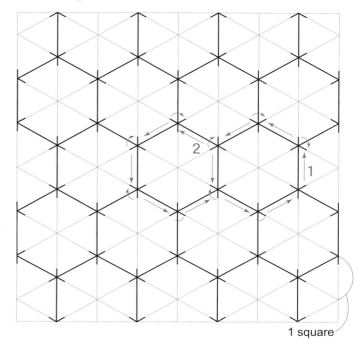

1 square

Woodblocks
積木 (TSUMIKI)

Regularly stacked blocks and diagonal crosses form the pattern. Stitch vertically up (1) and down (2), and then horizontally to the left (3) and right (4). When stitching diagonal lines 5 and 6, do not pull the fabric as it is easily stretched in bias direction.

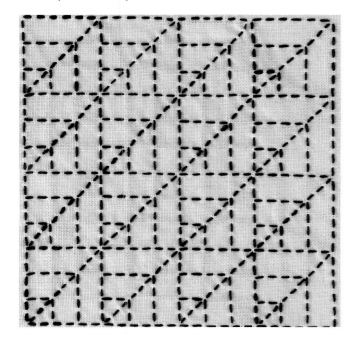

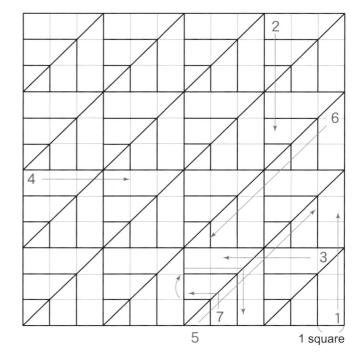

1 square

Rice Patch
詰田 (TSUMETA)

The character "田" depicts sorted rice patches, and this pattern is a sequence of such blocked patches divided by walking paths. Work long, vertical (1) and horizontal (2) lines first, and stitch the outer square followed by the inner square including the cross.

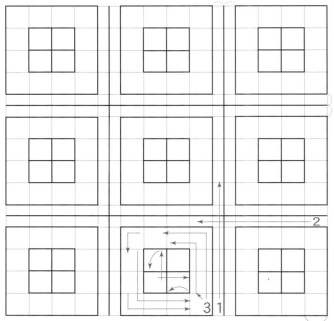

1 square

Tilted Cross
流し十字
(NAGASHI-JUJI)

One side of the cross is elongated, and the design is deformed by tilting the whole. Although crosses seem to be separately stitched, the longer line 1 is worked diagonally all through, and then the shorter line 2 in the other direction.

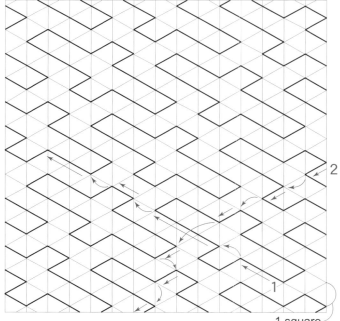

1 square

Tilted Linked Crosses
斜め方眼つなぎ
(NANAME-HOGAN-TSUNAGI)

Linked Crosses (page 14) are arranged in a diagonal pattern. The stitching method is the same as the original, working a long diagonal seam turning frequently. Begin with upward line 1, then downward 2.

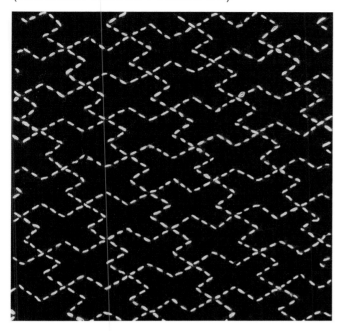
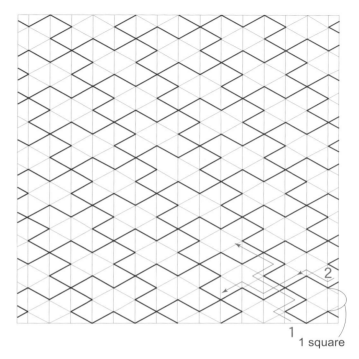

1 square

Double Tortoise Shell
二重亀甲つなぎ
(NIJU-KIKKO-TSUNAGI)

Right hexagons encase narrow hexagons in this variant of *kikko*. First, stitch zigzag lines 1 sideways, and then vertical lines 2, finishing with the side of the narrow hexagon (3), cutting and finishing off the thread after each seam.

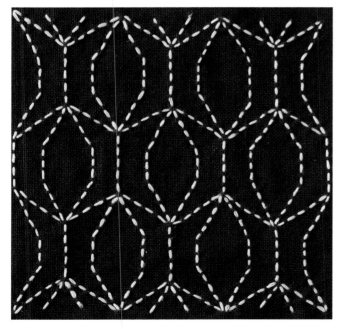
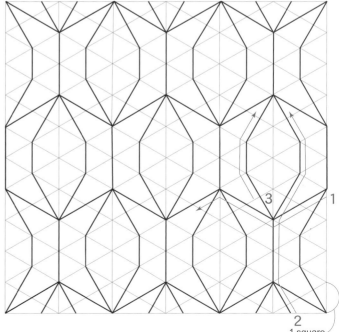

1 square

Tilted Well Frame
菱井桁 (HISHI-IGETA)

The character " 井 " is tilted and linked with the same but smaller designs in this version. It is important to avoid stitching into previous seams as there are lots of intersections. Adjust the stitch lengths as you go.

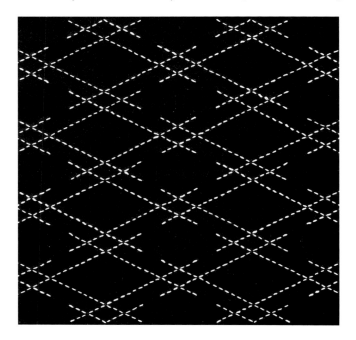

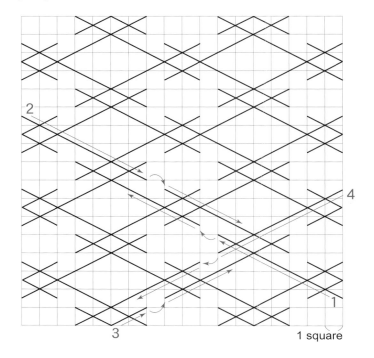

1 square

Diamond Ocean Waves
菱青海波 (HISHI-SEIGAIHA)

A straight-line version of "Ocean Waves" on page 40, having a three-dimensional effect depending on how you look at. Stitch the largest diamond by working long diagonal lines 1 to 4, and stitch the inner, angled lines 5 next.

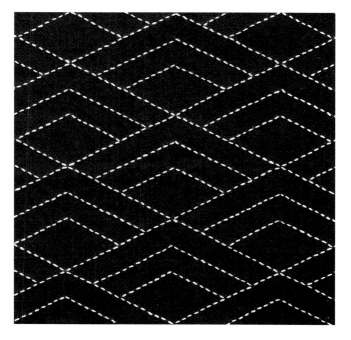

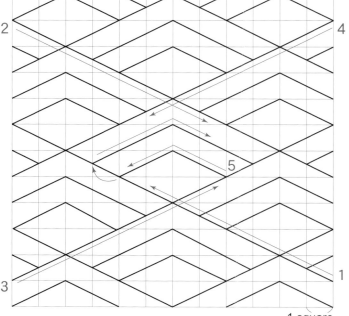

1 square

Diamond Swastika
菱卍 (HISHI-MANJI)

Although it is hard to see, the intersections of parallelograms show tilted swastikas in this *manji* pattern. Stitch long diagonals 1 and 2 to make the outer diamonds, and then the inner diamonds 3 as shown, connecting to the adjacent inner diamonds.

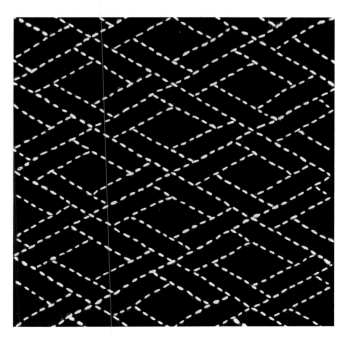

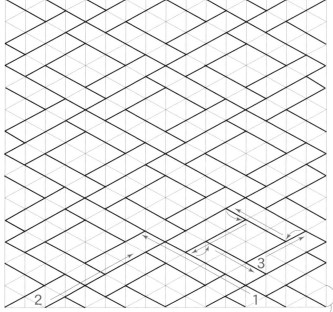

1 square

Diamond
菱模様 (HISHI-MOYO)

A basic, simple pattern consisting of the same size diamonds. As with all the similar patterns, be careful not to stretch the fabric when pulling it between your fingers for even tension of the thread.

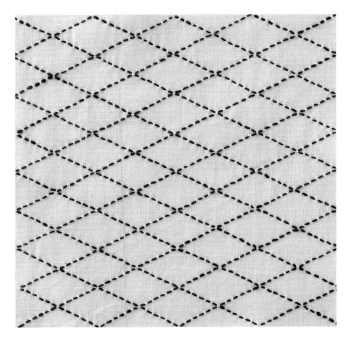

1 square

Doubled Well Frame
比翼井桁 (HIYOKU-IGETA)

Hiyoku means a double layer of fabric used in garments. In this *igeta* variant, squares overlap each other at the corners where straight lines run through in both directions. Work vertical and horizontal lines 1 and 2 to form a "graph", and stitch one square at a time.

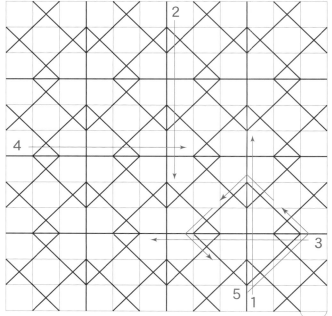

1 square

Triple-Line Cross
平井十文 (HIRAI-JUMON)

The character " 井 " is again duplicated resembling a cross of three parallels. Stitch one pattern at a time: Work vertical lines continuously, then connect to horizontal lines 2. Stitch carefully at intersections so as not to overlap with the previous stitch. Adjust the stitch lengths as you work.

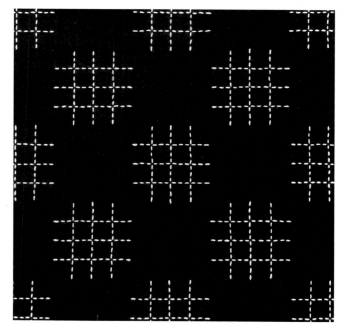

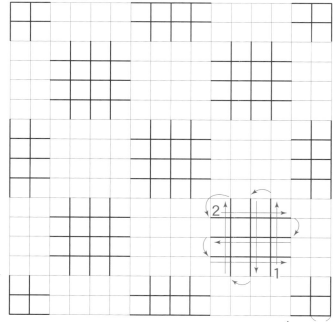

1 square

Linked Swastikas
平組卍つなぎ
(HIRAKUMI-MANJI-TSUNAGI)

The center square is surrounded with squares partially interlocking each other in this unique design. Swastika in Sanskrit script meaning good deeds and peace, it was introduced to Japan as a sign of good omen long ago. Stitch line 1, followed by line 2.

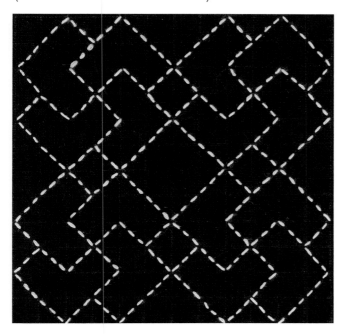

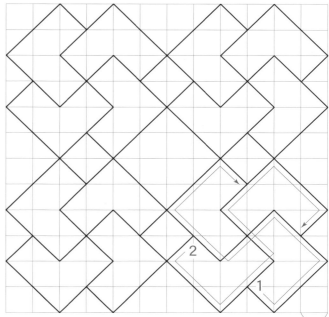

1 square

Simplified Paving Blocks
平三崩し (HIRA-SAN-KUZUSHI)

An arrangement of stripes resembling narrow sticks that are set up in a check pattern. "San" represents divining sticks, and in this pattern four blocks of three sticks are assembled next to a blank square. Stitch vertical lines 1 and then horizontal lines 2. Divide the square in half vertically (3) and horizontally (4). Divide each square into three, stitching 5 and 6.

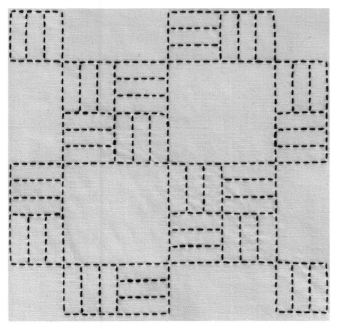

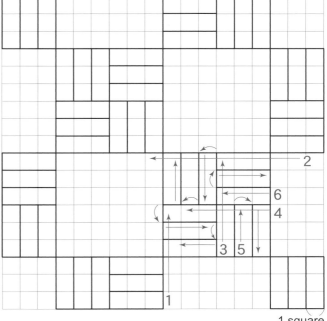

1 square

Mountain Passes
平山道
(HIRA-YAMA-MICHI)

A simple pattern of sideways lines only, turning alternately up and down. Be careful to stitch each side perpendicular to its partner, and stitch into the pivot points.

1 square

Three Nested Boxes
平詰三枡
(HIRATSUME-MIMASU)

"*Mimasu*", or three (*mi*) measuring boxes (*masu*) seen from above, is the crest of *kabuki* theater family, Ichikawa Danjuro being its legendary figure. Here the boxes are neatly set in divided sections. Make a "graph" of stitches 1 to 4, and then stitch the three boxes 5 inwards.

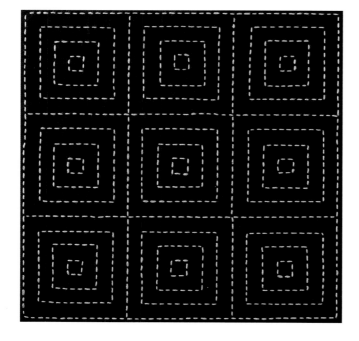

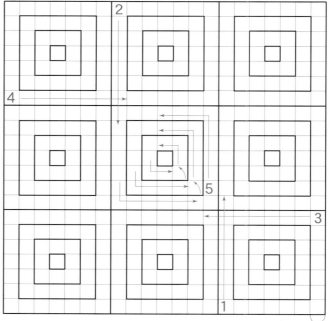

1 square

Fence Weave
檜垣 (HIGAKI)

This used to be one of the special patterns for the aristocracy. Wide slats of fragrant Japanese cypress were closely woven in a lattice pattern to make this *higaki* fence. Stitch diagonally upward first (1), turning back to stitch to the other direction.

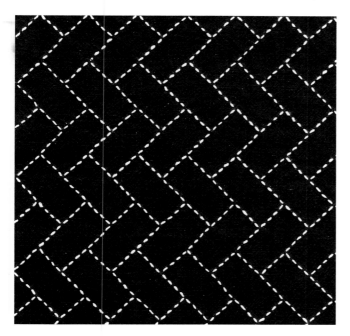

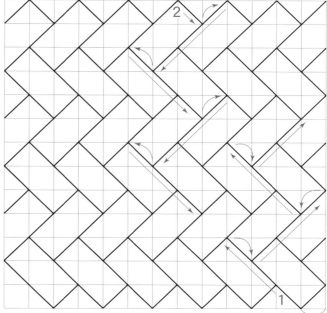

1 square

Bishamon
毘沙門亀甲
(BISHAMON-KIKKO)

Bishamon is one of the Seven Deities of Good Fortune, and this design was taken from his armor pieces which resembled the tortoise shell pattern. Three elongated tortoise shells are joined at two sides each to make the motif. As there is not a required working order, use one that is convenient for you.

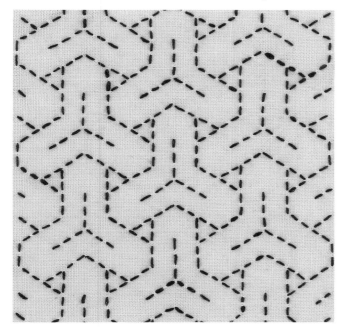

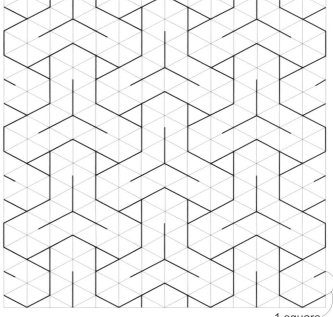

1 square

25

Measuring Boxes
枡刺し (MASU-SASHI)

Four wooden measuring boxes are nested and seen from above. The corners of these squares show a little difference from Three Nested Boxes on page 24. Stitch vertical lines 1 and 2, horizontal lines 3 and 4 across, followed by four squares. Stitch the outer square, and continue to the inner squares without breaking the thread. Pass thread on backside at corners.

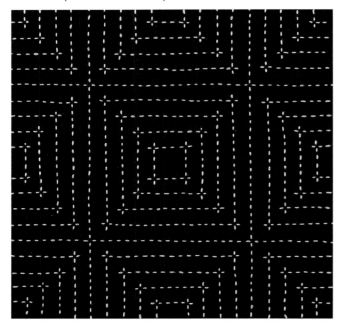

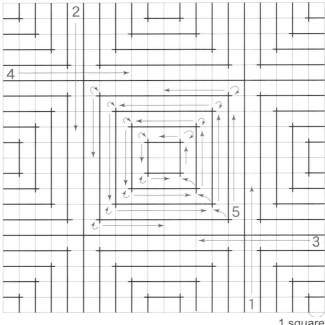

1 square

Pine Bark
松皮菱
(MATSUKAWA-HISHI)

A small diamond is added to the top and bottom of a large diamond, resembling a crackled bark of pine in it, hence the name. This is also a popular pattern in *kimono*, and unexpectedly easy to work. Stitch one line each, forming zigzag diagonally upward (1) and then downward (2).

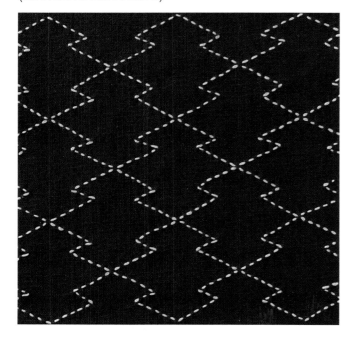

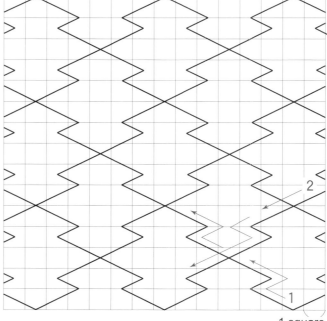

1 square

Facing Tortoise Shells
向かい亀甲 (MUKAI-KIKKO)

Tortoise shells are facing and interlocking each other in this variation. Begin with vertical line 1 passing the thread on the backside to continue upwards. Work zigzag lines 3 and 4, then the *kikko* lines 5 and 6.

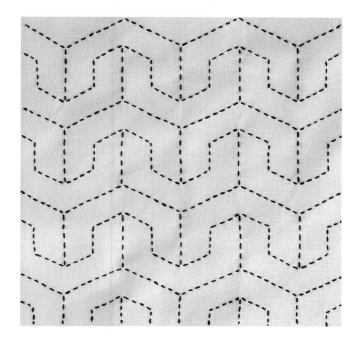

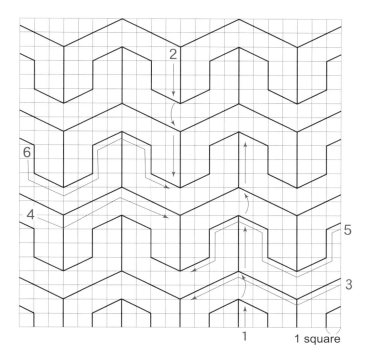

Linked Tortoise Shells
結び亀甲 (MUSUBI-KIKKO)

The straight sides of the small hexagon are extended to link to the adjacent hexagon, creating triangles in between. Stitch one triangle at a time, turning back to the tip of triangle by passing the thread on the backside.

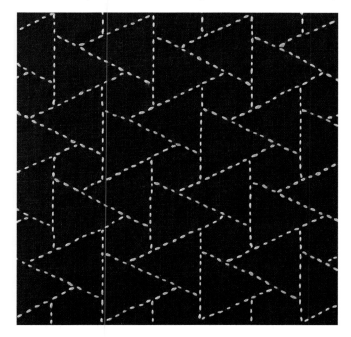

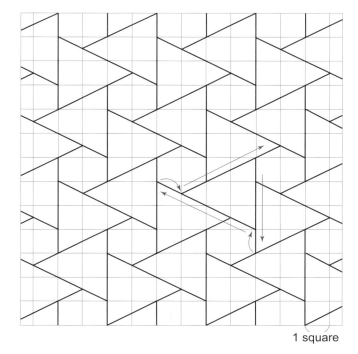

Arrow Feathers
矢羽根 (YABANE)

Arrow feathers are facing each other in this *kimono* pattern. Even now we often see female college students wearing *yabane* pattern *kimono* in purple and white at graduation ceremonies. This wide version can be altered by doubling the diagonal lines. Begin with steps up (1) and down (2), followed by diagonal lines 3 and 4.

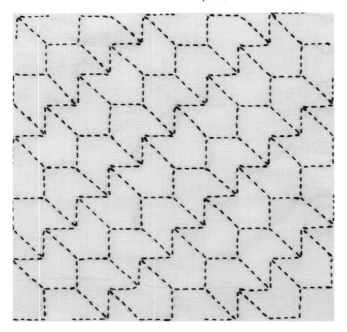

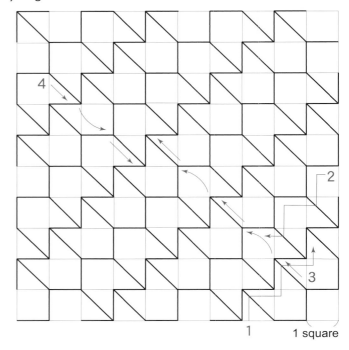

1 square

Parquetry
寄木 (YOSEGI)

This pattern creates an optical illusion resembling three-dimentional woodblocks. Since there are so many intersections, avoid overlapping the stitches as you go. As with other sashiko stitches, begin with vertical line (1) upward, and downward (2), then sideways (3 and 4) in a zigzag.

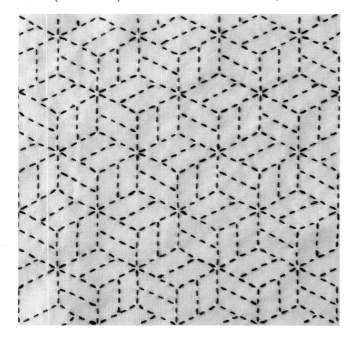

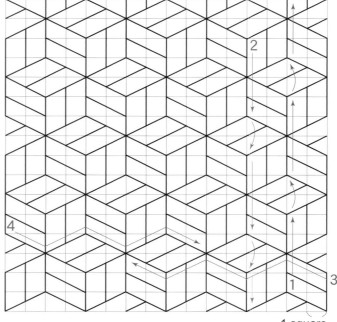

1 square

Overlapped Diamonds
四つ組菱 (YOTSUKUMI-HISHI)

The same sized diamonds are slightly overlapping at corners, forming tiny diamonds. Simply stitch one large diamond at a time. As there is lots of turning, make the points as clear-cut as possible by adjusting the stitch lengths so stitches meet in the corners.

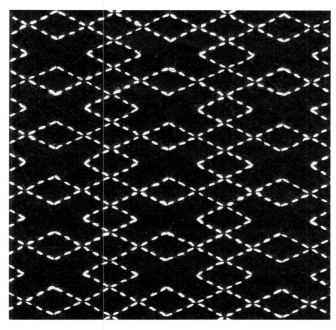

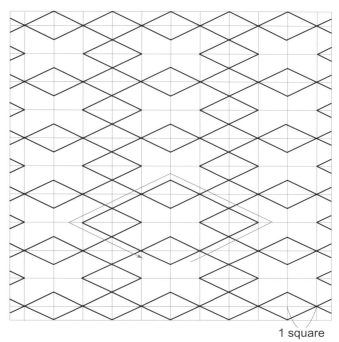

1 square

Thunderbolt
雷文 (RAIMON)

This basic thunderbolt pattern emphasizes horizontal lines. Begin with the straight line 1 across the fabric, and the hooked line 2 in the same direction. Stitch vertically across, passing the thread on the backside to continue without breaking the thread.

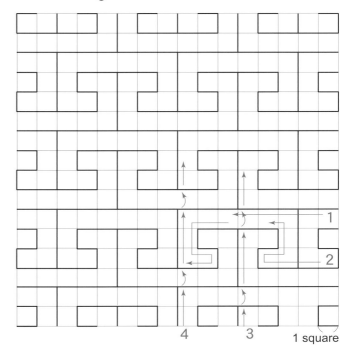

1 square

29

SASHIKO PROJECTS USING LINEAR PATTERNS

1+ Tote with DIAMOND OCEAN WAVES
Instructions on page 69
Finished Size: 25cm (10"x 10") with 8cm (3 1/4") gusset

Backside

2+ Drawstring Bag with THUNDERBOLT
Instructions on page 74
Finished Size: 21cm (8 1/4")W x 26cm(10 1/6")H

+ + + + + + +
The diagonal lines of ocean waves contrast well with the simple shape of the tote while neat thunderbolt stitches decorate the practical drawstring bag. Here a cotton thread in mixed blue hues is used for both.

+ + + + + + +

Hemp Leaf pattern is encased in a circle on one side and in a diagonal flow on the other side. Note both sides of the diagonal design have fading-out effect. This is done by decreasing stitch length as you work outwards. Pale green thread is used on an indigo dyed fabric.

3+ Table Runner with HEMP LEAF

Instructions on page 68
Finished Size: 100cm (40")W x 23cm (9")H

4+ Floor Cushion Covers with KEY PATTERN
Instructions on page 70
Finished Size: 46cm(18")W x 43cm (17)H

+ + + + + + +
A cherry blossom is stitched in the center of both cushions. The contrast of dark indigo and white enhances any interior.

5+ Floor Cushion Covers with HEMP LEAF
Instructions on page 70
Finished Size: 46cm(18)W x 43cm (17") H

6+ Place Mats with PAVING BLOCKS

Instructions on page 71
Finished Size: 50cm(20")W x 36cm(14 1/6")L

+ + + + + + +

The Paving Blocks are stitched in a strip on one side only, and the motif is on one corner like a crest.

+ + + + + + +

Mountains Passes are stitched in 3 rows and 6 rows separately, creating a modern impression.

7+ Doorway Curtain with MOUNTAIN PASSES
Instructions on page 73
Finished Size: 71cm(28")W x 122cm(48")L

8+ Tapestry with MOUNTAIN SHAPES

Instructions on page 72
Finished Size: 105cm(41 1/2")W x 105cm(41 1/2")L

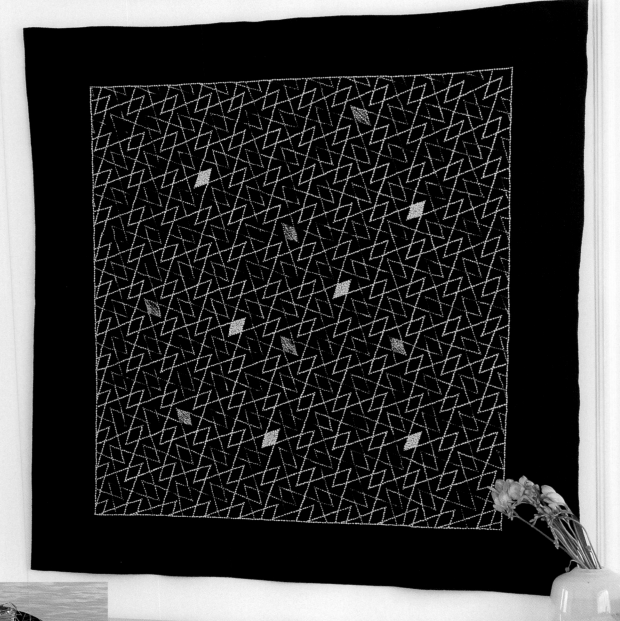

Enlarge to
make a table
cloth.

+ + + + + + +

Using two different mixed threads of white and
blue, Mountain Pass design is diagonally positioned
in a square frame. Fill several diamonds with
running stitches to give accents.

+ + + + + +

Utilizing the Key Pattern lines, six-pointed stars are added partially for this distinctive throw. Triple stitching lines give depth to the stars.

9+ **Throw with KEY PATTERN VARIATION**
Instructions on page 76
Finished Size: 138cm(54 1/2")W x 146cm(57 1/2")L

Gentle curving stitches of sashiko give a pleasant sense of movement to plain fabrics. Work carefully to create smooth flowing lines with uniform stitches. Also, when adjusting the thread tension, do not pull the fabric too tightly as it is easily stretched on the bias direction.

CURVED PATTERNS

Fishnet
網目 (AMIME)

This rhythmical design with up and down curves is known as FISHNET, literally meaning "network". Its history stretches back to ancient times. In the Edo Period (1600-1868) it became a favorite pattern for everyday items such as *kimono*, pottery and stone lanterns. Stitch one curving line sideways at a time.

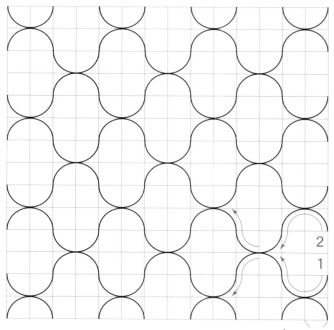

2

1

1 square

Mist
霞つなぎ
(KASUMI-TSUNAGI)

Drifting and swirling mist was stylized like this, and has been used as a background of many scrolls and *kimono* in Japan. Insert a row of narrow grids every 6th row to add interest. The overall impression can be altered by adjusting the x-curves.

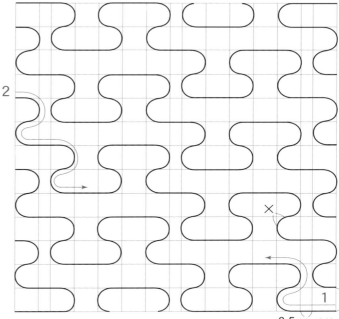

0.5 square
1 square

Seven Treasures
七宝 (SHIPPO)

This, as well as Hemp Leaf, is another symbolic sashiko design. Although it is often introduced as Seven Treasures, it seems an old name of this pattern was "*Jippo*", or all directions, resembling the sound of "*shippo*" which evokes the lucky image of seven jewels. Stitch in a waving pattern inwards.

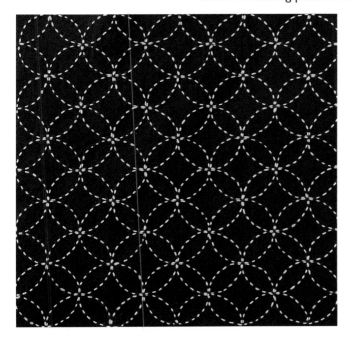

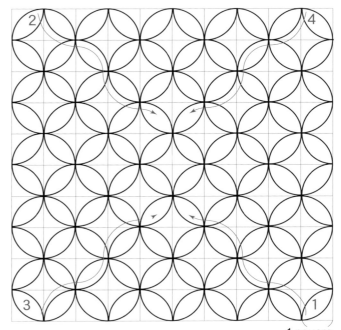

1 square

Ocean Waves
青海波 (SEIGAIHA)

"Seigaiha" is one of the well-known Japanese court music and dance pieces, and it is said this pattern first appeared in its costume. Concentric circles overlap to depict swirling sea waves. Taller or wider waves can be created by altering the grids into thin or wide rectangles. Stitch in order of the numbers, from the outer curve inwards.

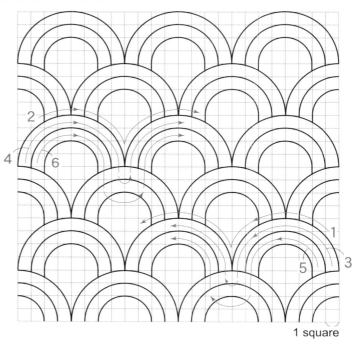

1 square

Linked Plovers
千鳥つなぎ
(CHIDORI-TSUNAGI)

This pattern depicts a flock of birds flying in the sky. *Chidori* literally means a thousand birds, which suggests they fly in large flocks. As the combination of semicircles run vertically and horizontally, repeat stitching vertical curves 1 and 2, and then 3 and 4 sideways. Enjoy variations by adjusting the size of x.

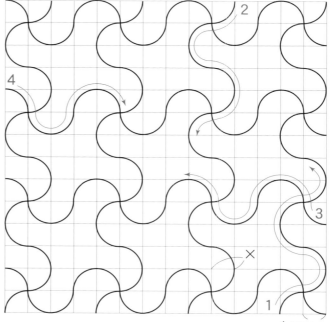

1 square

Rising Steam
立涌 (TATEWAKU)

Simple design expressing warm steam rising in gentle curves. This ancient *kimono* pattern developed into more decorative versions encasing plant motifs with doubled or tripled lines for members of the royal court since the Heian Period (794-1192). Repeat stitching upward and downward to avoid distortion. Adjust the size of x for variations.

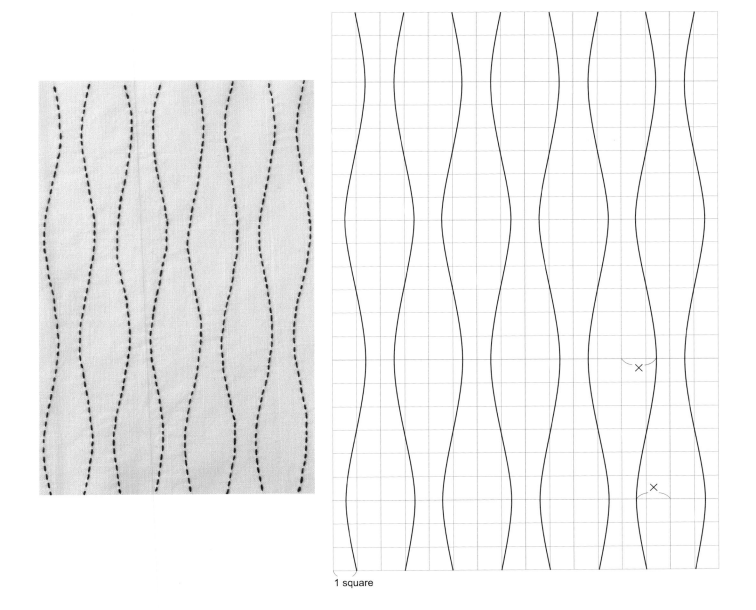

1 square

Crisscross Birds
鳥襷 (TORI-TASUKI)

A simpler version of LINKED PLOVERS, resembling a stylized *tasuki*, the long sleeves of *kimono* tucked up with a cord crossed in the middle. This pattern has gentler curves than other curved line patterns, and is easy to stitch. Work in the same manner as Linked Plovers on page 40.

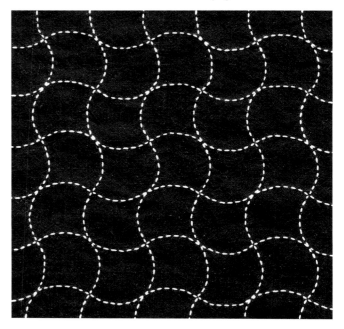

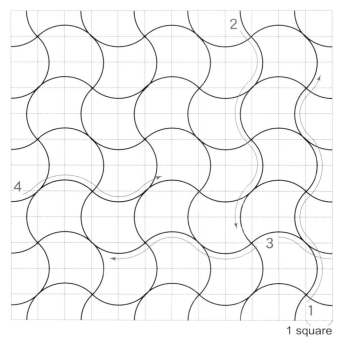

1 square

Linked Semicircles
半丸つなぎ
(HANMARU-TSUNAGI)

One large semicircle is combined with a pair of half-size semicircles, and faces other motifs at various angles. Stitch large semicircles 1 horizontally across the fabric, and vertically (2), followed by pairs of small semicircles 3 across. Repeat with semicircles 4.

1 square

Linked Counter Weights
分銅 (FUNDO)

This pattern can be seen in three ways: 1. The Japanese balanced weights have an hourglass shape, and they are linked in both directions. 2. Meandering lines intersect each other. 3. Tilted 卍 (swastika) motifs are linked together. Stitch diagonally upward, downward, and sideways. By altering the length of x, even more images are possible.

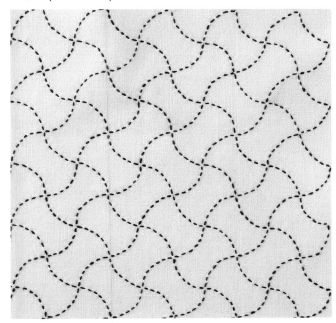

1 square

Rounded Bishamon
丸毘沙門
(MARU-BISHAMON)

Bishamon, a Tortoise Shell variant on page 25, is drawn with circles which are partially stitched. Using a diagonal grid paper, work one circle at a time, passing the thread on the backside to continue all around.

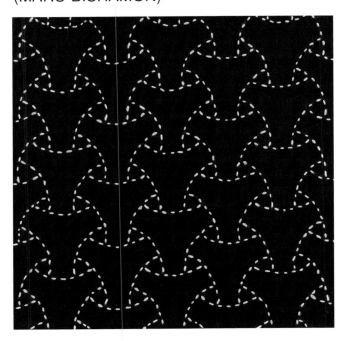

2 square
3 square

43

SASHIKO PROJECTS USING CURVED PATTERNS

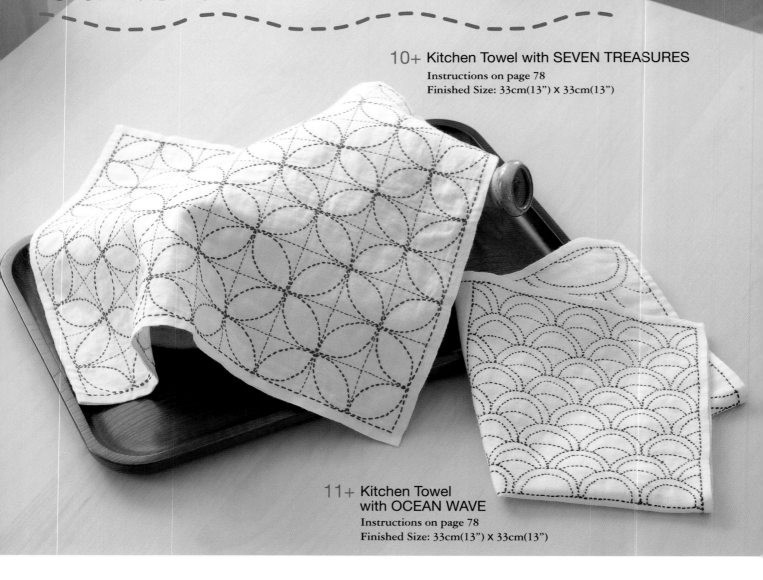

10+ Kitchen Towel with SEVEN TREASURES
Instructions on page 78
Finished Size: 33cm(13") x 33cm(13")

11+ Kitchen Towel
with OCEAN WAVE
Instructions on page 78
Finished Size: 33cm(13") x 33cm(13")

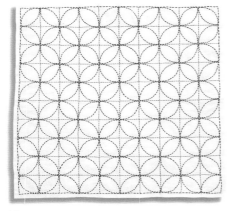

+ + + + + +

Lovely kitchen towels stitched in wine red and indigo blue over coarsely woven pure white cotton. SEVEN TREASURES pattern is worked all over while OCEAN WAVE is placed partially, varied in scale.

12+ Table Runner with FISHNET

Instructions on page 75
Finished Size: 27cm(10 1/2")W x 100cm(40")L

+ + + + + + +

The fishnet pattern is placed diagonally
and partial motif shows the appealing
the beauty of indigo and white contrast.
Such a gentle design will enhance any
type of room.

+ + + + + +

A wider than usual SEVEN TREASURES motif is arranged on a floor cushion. Note the colors of thread and the cushion fabric are in the same hue of yellowish green.

13+ Floor Cushion Covers with SEVEN TREASURES Variation
Instructions on page 75
Finished Size: 59cm(23 1/4")W x 63cm(25")L

14+ Tote with SEVEN TREASURES

Instructions on page 80
Finished Size: 33cm(13")H x 33cm(13")
W (Bottom) x 3cm(1 1/6") Gusset

15+ Tote with PLOVERS

Instructions on page 80
Finished Size: 32cm(12 1/2")H x 32cm(12 1/2")
W (Bottom) x 4cm(1 6/10") Gusset

+ + + + + + +
SEVEN TREASURES is stitched in a triangle using
white thread while PLOVERS are placed as a wide
strip over the bag. Endless designs can be created by
varying layout, shades and size of pattern.

SINGLE STITCH PATTERNS

In this category, one side is done in a single stitch. Decide the stitch length and keep it coustant all over the fabric. The most comfortable stitch length that is easy to balance is around 0.5cm(1/6"+) because longer threads may get caught and pulled out, causing distortion.

Hemp Leaf
麻の葉 (ASANOHA)

HEMP LEAF, presented on page 3, is downscaled to single stitch pattern. On 0.5cm-grid graph paper, draw 0.8 cm lines for the longest stitches, 0.6cm for the short stitches. Leave 0.2cm space for the center of each leaf. Stitch continuously following the numbers.

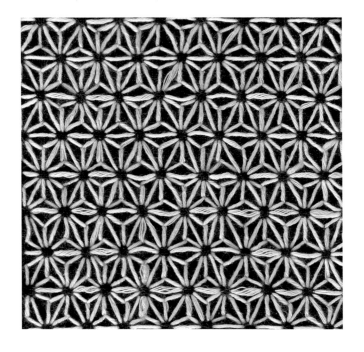

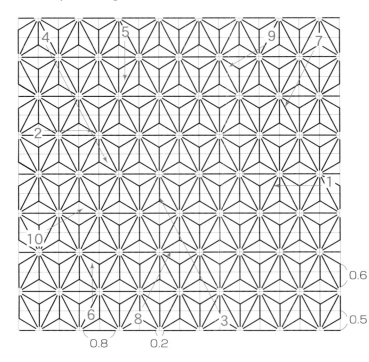

Persimmon Blossom
柿の花 (KAKI-NO-HANA)

Center squares are surrounded by zigzag squares in this old pattern. In fact, seams are done in straight running stitches that show dashes. Work vertically across the fabric and return. Repeat until all vertical seams are done, and then work sideways in the same manner.

Bamboo Basket
篭目 (KAGOME)

The regular BAMBOO BASKET pattern presented on page 7 is downsized by shortening each side to a single stitch. The result is a very realistic basket weave. Work vertically upward and downward, then diagonally toward right and left.

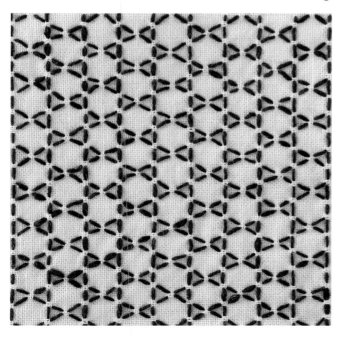

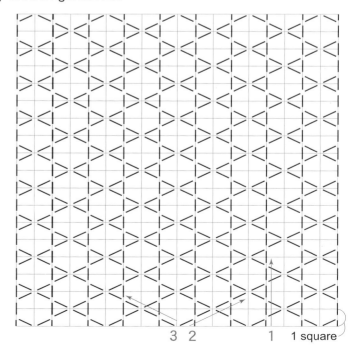

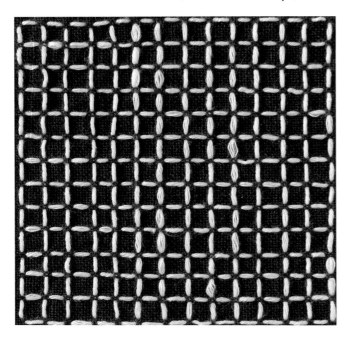

Checks
格子 (KOSHI)

The most basic design of single stitch sashiko. Although it looks easy, such a plain pattern will show any imperfection. Keep stitching uniform. Stitch vertically upward and downward. Repeat until all vertical lines are done, then stitch sideways, to left and right alternately.

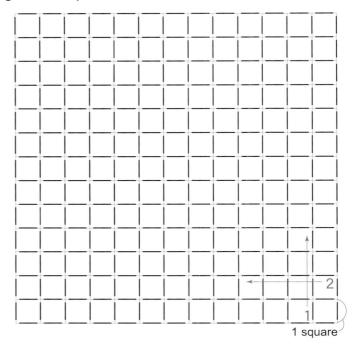

Rice Symbol
米刺し (KOME-SASHI)

The character 米 (*kome*) means rice, a staple food for the Japanese, and its shape resembles an asterisk. The characters are lined up in a lattice pattern.

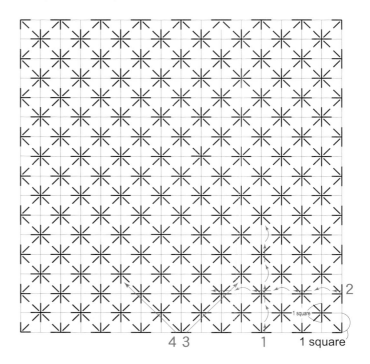

Single Stitch Patterns

Cross in Floret
十字花刺し
(JUJI-HANA-SASHI)

Tiny, elongated hexagons are combined to form a cross diagonally, and each space is also filled with a cross, creating a vivid design.

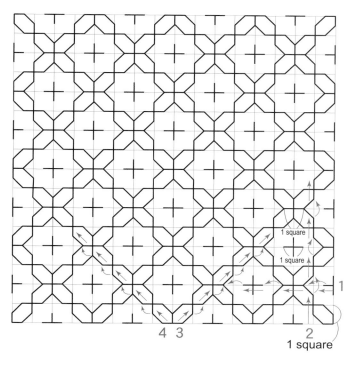

Coin
銭形刺し
(ZENIGATA-SASHI)

Another optical illusion pattern, linked ancient coins. First, work vertically and horizontally to stitch the squares, and then work diagonally in both directions, connecting the corners of each square by a single stitch.

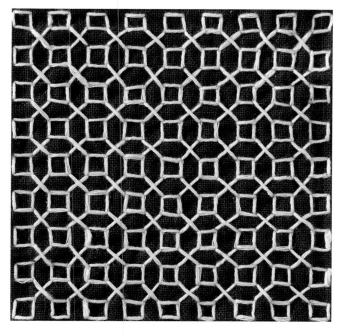

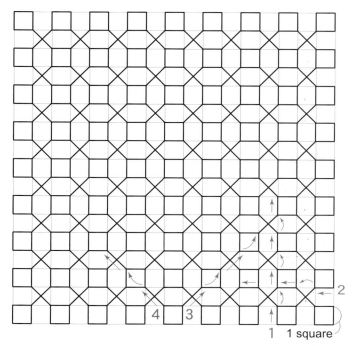

Floret
花刺し (HANA-SASHI)

Tiny stitches fill the entire fabric evenly as if little flowers are blooming all over. Work vertical lines 1 upward and downward, then work sideways (2) in the same manner. Stitch vertical lines 3 and 4 in both directions.

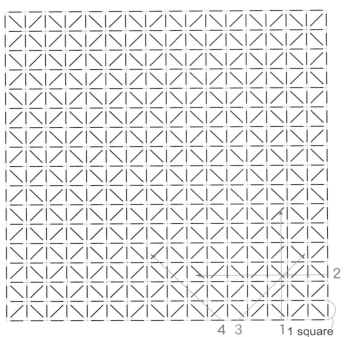

Arrow Feather
矢羽根 (YABANE)

A single stitch version of ARROW FEATHERS presented on page 28. Work vertically and horizontally across the fabric. Repeat until all vertical lines are done. Then work diagonal lines. Be sure to leave no space between stitches.

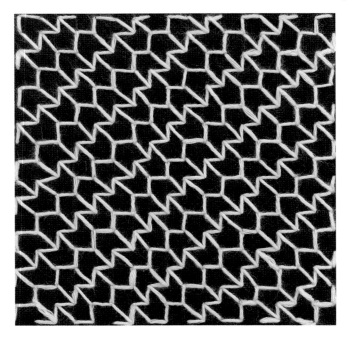

SASHIKO PROJECTS USING SINGLE STITCH PATTERNS

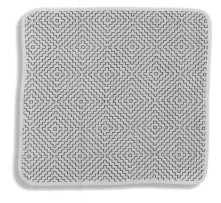

+ + + + + + +

Layer two pieces of coarsely woven cotton, and stitch through the layers. In 16, there are four diamonds while in 17 there are three diamonds. Purchased double-fold bias tape is used to bind the edges.

16+ Kitchen Towel with PERSIMMON BLOSSOM
Instructions on page 82
Finished Size: 34.5cm(13 6/10") W
x 33cm(13")L

17+ Kitchen Towel with PERSIMMON BLOSSOM
Instructions on page 82
Finished Size: 34.5cm(13 6/10") W
x 33cm(13")L

18+ Drawstring Bag with FLORET
Instructions on page 85
Finished Size: 10cm(4")W
x 23cm(9")L

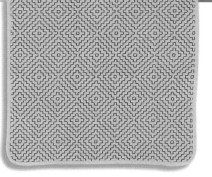

+ + + + + + +

Arranged FLORET pattern stitched with orange and white threads. The height of the design is changed on the backside.

Transferring Patterns

Use a water soluble chalk paper or chalk of similar color to the fabric to avoid any visible line when finished. You can draw the pattern directly on the fabric.

1 On the right side of the fabric, place chalk paper colored side down, checking the design position.

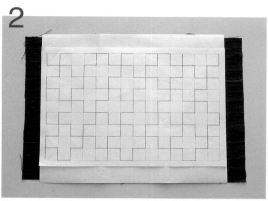

2 Place the traced pattern on top of the chalk paper.

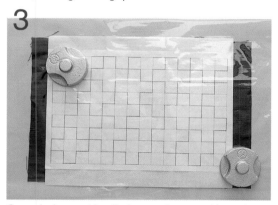

3 Cover the layers with cellophane, and secure with weights to avoid slippage.

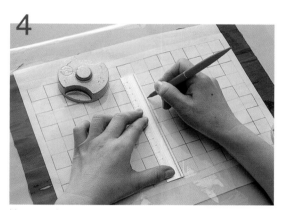

4 Using a stylus, trace the pattern with a help of a ruler for straight lines.

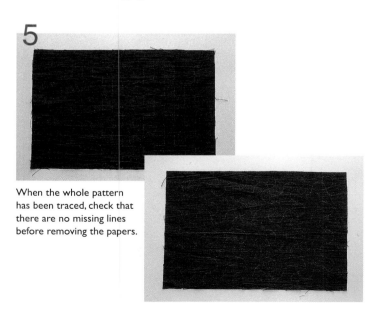

5 When the whole pattern has been traced, check that there are no missing lines before removing the papers.

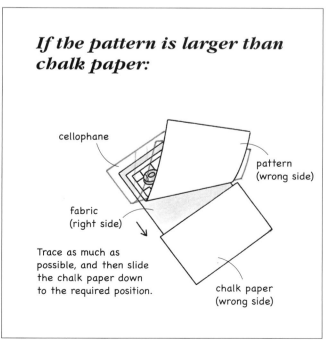

If the pattern is larger than chalk paper:

cellophane

pattern (wrong side)

fabric (right side)

chalk paper (wrong side)

Trace as much as possible, and then slide the chalk paper down to the required position.

Positioning Designs

Here is how to decide the size and the position of the design when making a sashiko project. Whether chosen from linear, curved or single stitch patterns, the method stays the same.

1 *Decide the pattern and its placement*

First, consider where you want to place the sashiko design in proportion to the project size. At this point the grid size you will use for pattern drawing has not been decided, and so the finished size may somewhat differ from the plan. Measure length X and width Y.

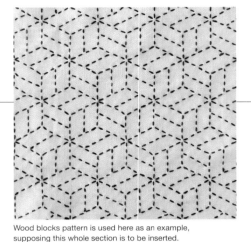

Wood blocks pattern is used here as an example, supposing this whole section is to be inserted.

2 Decide how many motifs you want to include in the sashiko area, lengthwise. On a piece of paper, draw the size of the area to contain the motif, and at the center draw one motif as shown below. This becomes the center of the design.

Position the same number of motifs above and below the center motif. Decide how may motifs can be included vertically. There are two ways to insert sashiko section: Type A has unstitched borders whereas in type B the whole area is stitched as if a continuous pattern has been cut out. Choose the type you prefer and check the number of motifs in order to calculate the grids. Count spacing grids if positioning at an interval.

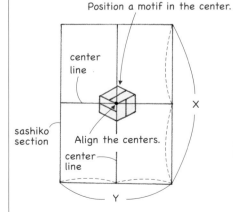

Three Positioning Styles:

with intervals   overlapping   mitering

For example, in type B when you include 3 motifs vertically, count how many grids are necessary in X cm (inches).
Calculation for type B:
number of grids needed to a motif (4) x number of motifs (3) + number of unstitched grids (2x2=4) = 16 grids

3 *Calculate the size of grid for the graph paper.* ——— Divide length X by grid number ▲ (16):

Xcm(inches) ÷ grid number ▲ = grid size (★cm/inches)

The result often has some remainder, in which case calculate to one decimal place, and drop the remainder.

4 *Draw grids of the calculated size for the sashiko section. Draw triangular grids depending on the pattern.*

Calculate the number of horizontal grids.

Ycm(inches) ÷ grid number★ = horizontal grid number

Drop off any remainder to create a whole number. Sashiko patterns include one with center line, and the other without center line.

As it is quite hard to draw regular arcs for curved patterns, photocopy graph paper into a scaled size according to the calculated grid. Use either purchased graph paper or use the graph on page 87.

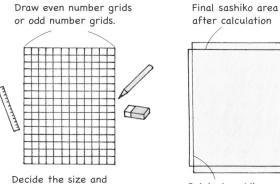

Pattern with center line: Even number grids

TRIPLE-LINE CROSSES

center line

PARQUETRY

center line

Pattern without center line: Odd number grids

LINKED CROSSES

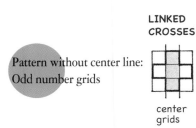

center grids

KEY PATTERN VARIATION

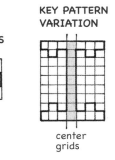

center grids

Draw even number grids or odd number grids.

Decide the size and number of grid, and draw necessary grids.

Final sashiko area after calculation

Original sashiko area planned in Step 2

If the sashiko area and design do not match:
Adjust the horizontal grid to either even number or odd number. Since it is natural that the original area and the grids do not match, adopt the drawn grids and alter the original area.

5 *Draw pattern over the grids, and check the sequence vertically and horizontally:*

Draw a motif in the center. Add more motifs in all directions. The pattern is well positioned if the added motifs count the same on each side of the center motif in both ways.

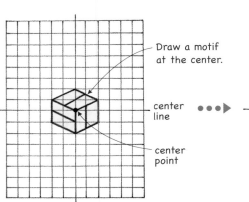

Draw a motif at the center.

center line

center point

center line

Add motifs upward and downward.

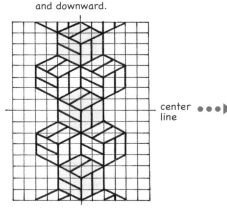

center line

Add motifs leftward and rightward.

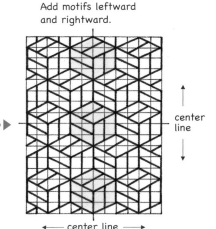

center line

center line

Stitching Sashiko —— About Needles, Fabrics and Threads

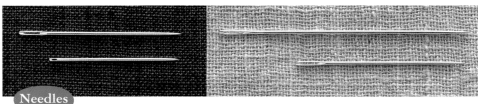

Needles

Fine needles: Used to stitch into fabrics with fine grains, or when using few strands of thread.

Thick and Long needles: Used for heavy or coarse grained fabrics, or when greater numbers of strands are threaded.

++++++++++++++++++++
++++++++++++++++++++

Fabrics

Thin fabric: In the above example, the left side seam is stitched with a single strand of thread whereas four strands are used for the right side seam. A single strand is appropriate for the fabric because the fabric ripples when a thick needle is threaded with several strands.

Thick fabric: In the above example, the left side seam is stitched with a single strand of thread whereas four strands are used for the right side seam. In this case, either will do. Use thick thread such as four strands for longer stitches.

Strands of thread

Thin needle: The eye of the needle is for one to two strands of thread. Best for fabrics of fine grains or soft fabric.

Thick needle: The eye of the needle is large enough to hold multiple strands of thread. Thick or coarse fabrics need this type of needle.

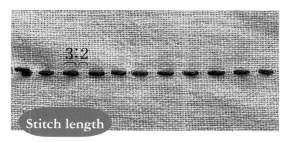

Stitch length

In sashiko, it is essential to keep the stitches on the surface longer than the ones on backside. A well-balanced ratio of surface stitch and backside stitch would be around 3:2. Be flexible and adjust the stitch lengths according to design, fabric and thread.

How to hold a needle and leather thimble

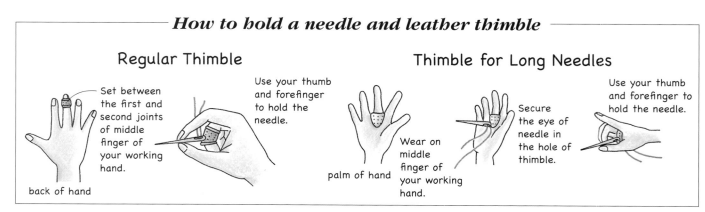

Regular Thimble

Set between the first and second joints of middle finger of your working hand.

back of hand

Use your thumb and forefinger to hold the needle.

Thimble for Long Needles

Wear on middle finger of your working hand.

palm of hand

Secure the eye of needle in the hole of thimble.

Use your thumb and forefinger to hold the needle.

Continuous Stitching and Flattening

To sew a straight running stitch, the Japanese use a special method called "*unshin*", or weaving stitch. With this method, a straight line can be sewn speedily in one stretch. You may need a little practice to get used to the movement:

1

Hold the fabric right side up, and take up a stitch.

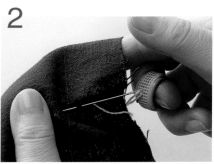

2

Fix eye of the needle in a hole of thimble, at a right angle. Always keep the angle of needle against the thimble.

3

Lightly hold the needle and fabric with your thumb and forefinger.

4

Pushing the needle down with your thumb, use the other hand to pull up the fabric and let the point of the needle go through. Keep the needle at a right angle to the thimble.

5

Keeping the needle at right angle to the thimble, push up the needle with the forefinger, at the same time pulling down the fabric with the other hand.

6

Repeat Steps 4 and 5 as if "weaving" through the fabric, always pushing the needle against the thimble to make uniform stitches.

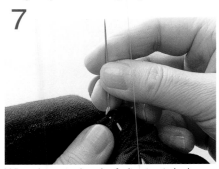

7

When the entire length of a line is stitched through, gently pull out the needle.

8

Pull the thread carefully until the slack at the beginning disappears.

9

Straighten the fabric : Gently holding the beginning stitch with one hand, pull the fabric between your thumb and other fingers toward the end of the line of stitches.

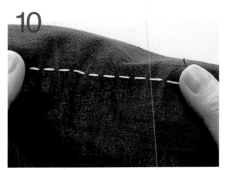

10

Showing the condition after one row of stitching. Repeat 2 to 3 times or more to smooth out the fabric.

11

+++++++++++++++++++++++++
+++++++++++++++++++++++++

A seam line completed.
Be sure to keep the
stitches uniform for a
neat finish.

BEGINNING AND END OF STITCHES

Securing with knot

This is the fastest way of securing thread ends. Since the knots will be visible, use this method only for lined projects.

1

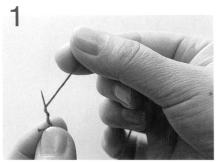

Hold threaded needle, pointed tip up. Grasping the end of the thread with your thumb and forefinger, wind the thread twice around the needle.

2

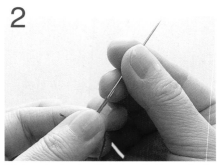

Pull down the thread, and hold the coil with your thumb. Pull up the needle until you feel the eye of needle meet the fabric, and then pull completely maintaining the grasp.

3

A knot is made. Cut off the tail close to the knot.

4

Insert the needle from the back side to front side. This is to secure the knot on the backside.

5

Wear a thimble. Referring to page 63, push the needle with the thimble at a right angle, at the same time pulling the fabric up and down.

6

When a line of sewing is done, pull the needle to the backside. Smooth out the fabric referring to page 63.

7

Place the needle at the point where you pulled it out. Grasping the needle with your thumb and forefinger, wind the thread twice around the needle.

8

Pull the needle, tightly grasping the coil with your thumb, until a knot is made. Cut off the thread tail close to the knot.

RIGHT SIDE

WRONG SIDE

When you run out of thread

Finish off by tying a knot on the backside. Restart stitching by tying a knot at the point of the next stitch.

Securing with backstitches

This method will avoid bulky knots, and so you can use it for a single layer sashiko embroidery.

1

Insert the needle from the back side to front, at three stitches from the beginning point. Sew three stitches backwards and pull the needle to the back side.

2

Turn the fabric around, and pull the thread leaving the thread tail about 1.5cm(1/2"). work 3 stitches backwards, inserting the needle just below the previous stitches.

3

Bring the needle up at the fourth stitch position. From this stitch, work continuous stitches (page 63), pushing the needle with the thimble.

4

When the entire leugth of the line is stitched through, gently pull out the needle.

5

Turn the fabric around, and stitch backwards by inserting the needle as close to the original stitches as possible, and hiding the thread underneath them on the right side.

6

Clip away the thread leaving 1.5cm(1/2") .When all the stitches are done, trim to 0.3cm(1/8") as well as the other thread tails.

How to begin stitching

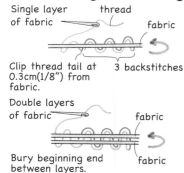

Single layer of fabric — thread — fabric

Clip thread tail at 0.3cm(1/8") from fabric.   3 backstitches

Double layers of fabric — fabric

Bury beginning end between layers. — fabric

How to end stitching

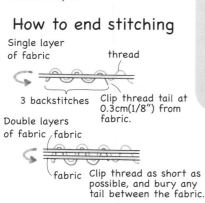

Single layer of fabric — thread

3 backstitches   Clip thread tail at 0.3cm(1/8") from fabric.

Double layers of fabric — fabric

Clip thread as short as possible, and bury any tail between the fabric. — fabric

Insert the needle with a new piece of thread from the wrong side, and work three stitches over the original stitches (so they hide just underneath when seen from the right side).

When you run out of thread

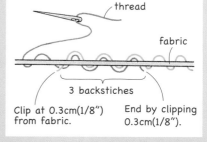

thread

fabric

3 backstiches

Clip at 0.3cm(1/8") from fabric.

End by clipping 0.3cm(1/8").

Bring the needle to the wrong side. Using a thimble, stitch continuously until a line is done. Pull out the needle on the wrong side, and smooth out the fabric.

RIGHT SIDE

WRONG SIDE

Linear Patterns

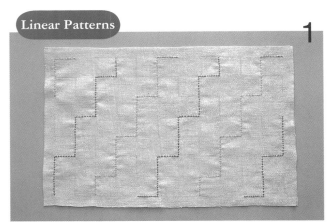

Work vertical lines first, forming "staircases" in this example. On each row, alternate working direction, e.g. upward and then downward.

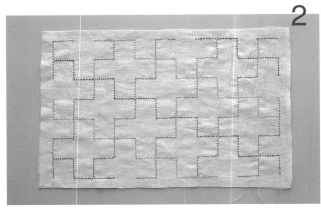

Stitch horizontal lines, forming "staircases" in this example. On each row, alternate working direction, back and forth.

Curved Patterns

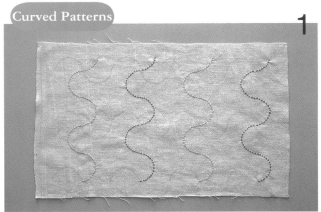

Work vertical lines first, forming "wave" pattern in this example. On each row, alternate working direction, e.g. upward and then downward.

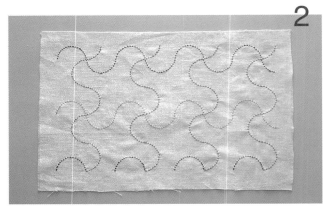

Work horizontal lines, in a wave pattern in this example. On each row, alternate working direction, back and forth.

Individual Patterns

Do not finish off thread at the end of each line. Pass thread to the nearest line, taking a little slack on the backing fabric to avoid too much tension. It is recommended to add backing fabric to your finished piece to cover these loose threads.

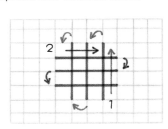

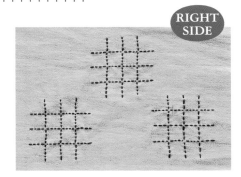

RIGHT SIDE

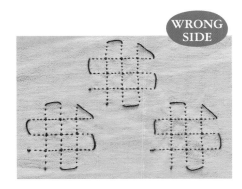

WRONG SIDE

STITCHING RULES

For best results, stitch carefully where two or more lines meet. Here are traditional methods to show that the corners are clear and even.

Pivot

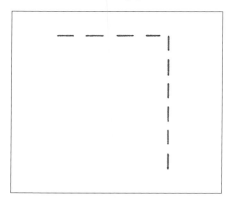

Insert the needle into the pivot, and bring it out taking as little space as possible. If taking a regular interval here, the corner will look blurry.

" T " shape

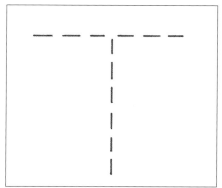

Do not stitch into the blank space of the original line, and end as close as possible to it.

Cross

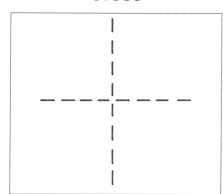

Never make a crossover stitch at any intersection, and leave the even seams.

Star

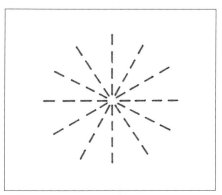

Leave the center unstitched so that the lines radiate from the circle. This also prevents a bulk on the backside.

Curve

A gentle curve can be stitched without a break just like working a straight line. Pull out the needle to the backside, and smooth out the fabric several times. When stitching a steep curve, pull out the needle after every few stitches, and smooth out the fabric gently each time. In both cases, make stitch width shoter, and be careful not to stretch the fabric when stroking the fabric.

FINISHING TOUCH

+++
+++

Ironing

If the pattern is traced with chalk paper, spray with water to erase before ironing. Do not press down with the iron on the stitches as they will be flattened. Hold the steam iron close to the fabric placed right side down, and just let the stitches and fabric relax.

right side of sashiko

Erase marking.   spray

wrong side of sashiko

Iron on the wrong side.

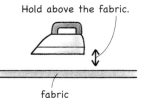

Hold above the fabric.

fabric

PROJECT INSTRUCTIONS

Use life-size patterns either by photocopying or tracing onto another sheet of paper.

#3 TABLE RUNNER
WITH "HEMP LEAF" --- shown on page 31

For life-size pattern Ⓑ, see supplement (Side A).
Materials
110cm (44") x 30cm(12") front fabric
110cm (44") x 30cm(12") backing
Yellow green cotton sashiko thread
Finished Size: 100cm(40") x 23cm(9")

LIFE-SIZE PATTERN Ⓐ

For design Ⓑ, copy or trace the supplement
life-size pattern (Side A).
Take 2 strands of sashiko thread.

CUTTING GUIDE

23 cm

TABLE RUNNER
Cut 1 each of front and backing fabric.

FRONT FABRIC
BACKING

—————— 100cm ——————

Add 1cm seam allowance and cut out.

SEWING GUIDE

(Stitch sashiko on front fabric before making up.)

Front fabric (Right Side)   machine stitches

BACKING (WRONG SIDE)   Leave 8-9cm as opening.

Turn over.

FRONT FABRIC (RIGHT SIDE)   Hem-stitch to close opening.

COMPLETION

For a natural fade-away effect,
gradually reduce stitch lenghs on right side.

33.5cm

yellow green sashiko thread   Ⓐ

16cm   Ⓑ   17.5cm

21cm   Measurements are not converted into inches for accuracy.

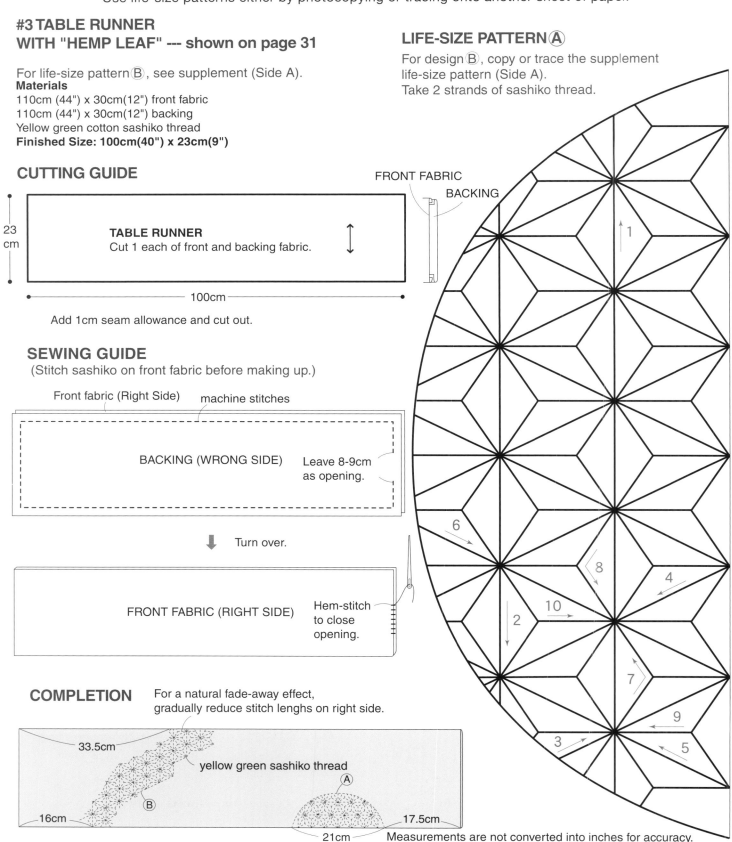

68

#1 TOTE WITH "DIAMOND OCEAN WAVES" ----shown on page 30

Life-Size Pattern on SUPPLEMENT (Side A)

Materials

70cm (28") x 70cm (28") indigo-died cotton fabric
40cm (16") x 60cm (24") quilted fabric for lining
30cm (12") x 20cm (8") cotton fabric for pocket
90cm (36") x 40cm (24") fusible interfacing
90cm (36") x 60cm (24") fusible batting
Sashiko threads: blue-gray and blue mix
Cardboard

Finished size:

25cm (10") height x 25cm (10") bottom width with 8cm (3 1/4") gusset

SEWING GUIDE

(Stitch sashiko only on the front before making up.)

HANDLE
(CUT 2 each outer fabric and fusible interfacing)

interfacing
0.2cm 0.5cm
1
2cm
fold
33cm

CUTTING GUIDE

LINING BAG

OUTER BAG

Handle attaching position
9cm
1
0.5cm
1
OUTER FABRIC (CUT 1)
FUSIBLE BATTING (CUT 1)
29cm
4cm
Quilting
2cm 4cm
4cm
4cm
fold
33cm

Fold facing only.
Handle attaching position
9cm
1
0.5cm
1
front fabric
3
2cm
14cm
POCKET (CUT 1)
cotton fabric
7cm
0.2cm
1
29cm
4cm
19cm
1
4cm
LINING (CUT 1)
fold
33cm

FACING (CUT 1)
interfacing
Facing
4.5cm
1.5cm front fabric
fusible batting
lining
4cm

Cut out with added seam allowance of circled number width (cm).

FACING
(CUT 1)

1
1. Attach fusible quilt batting, aligning with bag opening of finished size.

FUSIBLE BATTING

OUTER FABRIC (WRONG SIDE)

2. Machine-quilting

2
OUTER FABRIC (WRONG SIDE)

1. Machine-stitch.

FUSIBLE BATTING

Fold.

card
24cm
7cm

3. Machine-stitch.
2. Press seam open.
side
fusible batting
4cm 4cm
4. Sew gusset and place card onto bottom.

3
For pocket details, see page 74.
0.5cm   2.5cm
POCKET (RIGHT SIDE) 2cm
8cm
0.2cm
Attach inside
Machine-stitch.
LINING BAG (RIGHT SIDE)

4
HANDLE (RIGHT SIDE)
0.5cm
1. Stitch sashiko.
0.5cm

4. Machine-stitch.
(WRONG SIDE)
2. Attach fusible interfacing.
0.2cm 0.5cm
3. Fold.
(RIGHT SIDE)
5. Stitch sashiko.

Leave 7-8cm opening unsewn.

5
LINING (WRONG SIDE)
1. Machine-stitch.
Fold.

2. Press seam open.
LINING (WRONG SIDE)
side seam
4cm 4cm
3. Machine-stitch.

6
FACING (RIGHT SIDE)
2. Machine-stitch.
Fold.
FACING (WRONG SIDE)
3. Press seam open.
1. Attach fusible interfacing.

4. Machine-stitch.
LINING (WRONG SIDE)
FACING (WRONG SIDE)
LINING (RIGHT SIDE)
OUTER BAG (WRONG SIDE)

5. Fold seam allowance to facing.
FACING (RIGHT SIDE)

6. Sandwich handle.
7. Machine-stitch.
OUTER BAG (RIGHT SIDE)

LINING (RIGHT SIDE)
LINING (WRONG SIDE)

COMPLETION

OUTER BAG (RIGHT SIDE)
9. Machine stitch on right side.
0.5cm
LINING (RIGHT SIDE)
8. Work hem-stitch to close opening.

blue mix (2 strands)
blue gray (2 strands)
blue mix (1 strand)
Fill this segment with dense sashiko stitches.

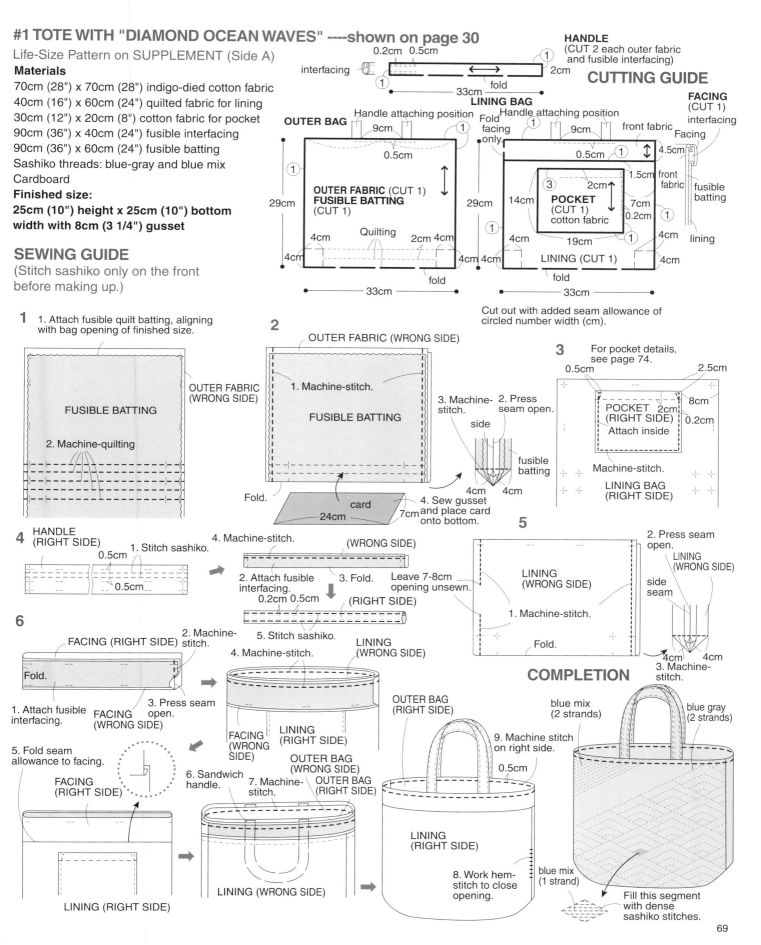

69

#4 /#5 FLOOR CUSHION COVERS WITH "KEY PATTERN" and "HEMP LEAF" --- shown on page 32

Life-Size Pattern on SUPPLEMENT (#4: Side A, #5: Side B)

Materials per each cover
110cm (44") x 50cm (20") cotton fabric
139cm (15 4/10") zip
White sashiko thread
Finished Size: 46cm (8 1/4") W x 43cm (10 1/6") H

CUTTING GUIDE FOR EACH #4 and #5

Cut out with added seam allowance of circled number width (cm).

- 1.5cm
- ① 1.5cm
- **BACK** | **BACK**
- Folding line | Folding line
- 43cm | 1cm | Zip opening | Zip opening
- ⑴.⑸
- **FRONT** (CUT 1)
- 1.5cm | ① 1.5cm
- ⑴.⑸
- 40cm ──── 46cm ──── 6cm

SEWING GUIDE

(Stitch sashiko only on the front before making up.)
Finish edges of seam allowance with serger or zigzag stitches.

1. Machine-stitch. (RIGHT SIDE)
2. Baste. (WRONG SIDE)
3. Machine stitching (WRONG SIDE)
1. Machine-stitch.
1cm below marking
Pull 0.3cm.
zip

4. Baste. (WRONG SIDE)
6. Remove basting. awl
1cm
5. Machine-stitch. (WRONG SIDE)

8. Machine-stitch.
7. Machine-stitch only on seam allowances.
Fold. (WRONG SIDE)
Fold.
zip
8. Machine-stitch.

COMPLETION OF #4

For stitching KEY PATTERN, see page 12.

Take 2 strands of sashiko thread unless specified.

FRONT 46cm — 43cm
white (1 strand)
French knot stitch

BACK

French Knot Stitch

out → 1.out 2.in

COMPLETION OF #5

For stitching HEMP LEAF, see page 3.

Take 2 strands of sashiko thread unless specified.

French knot stitch(white, 1 strand)
FRONT 46cm — 43cm
white (1 strand)

BACK

70

#6 PLACE MATS WITH "PAVING BLOCKS"
--- Shown on page 33

Materials per piece
110cm (44") x 40cm (16") cotton fabric
White sashiko thread

Finished Size: 50cm (20")W x 36cm (14 1/6")L

CUTTING GUIDE

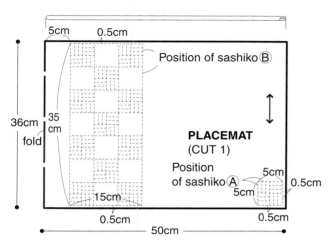

Cut out adding 1cm seam allowance all around.

SEWING GUIDE (Stitch sashiko only on the front, before making up.)

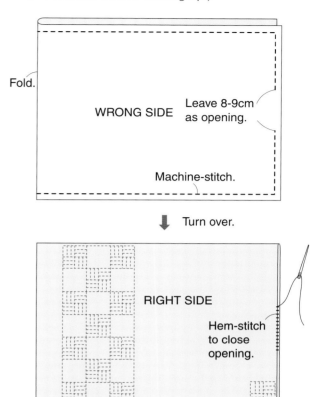

LIFE-SIZE SASHIKO PATTERN Ⓑ

Draw the whole design of 7 rows, by shifting this pattern.

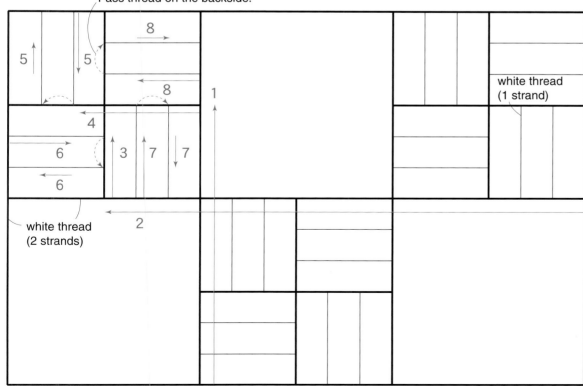

For sashiko pattern A, stitch one segment of this pattern.

#8 TAPESTRY WITH "MOUNTAIN SHAPES" --- shown on page 35

Materials
110cm (44") W x 120cm (47") L cotton fabric
White and blue-mix sashiko threads
Finished Size: 105cm (41") W x 105cm (41") L

CUTTING/STITCHING GUIDE

*Life-size pattern is not provided. To make the shown size tapestry, enlarge the pattern so that each gird measures 2.5cm, and transfer the design onto fabric.

* Cut out with added seam allowance of circled number width (cm).

*See page 16 for stitching MOUNTAIN SHAPES.

How to sew corners

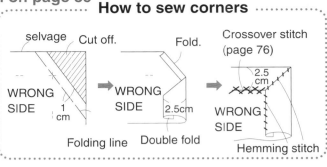

selvage   Cut off.   Fold.   Crossover stitch (page 76)

WRONG SIDE   1 cm

WRONG SIDE   2.5cm

2.5 cm

WRONG SIDE

Folding line   Double fold   Hemming stitch

Work dense sashiko stitches to fill the segment.
 : blue-mix
◆ : white

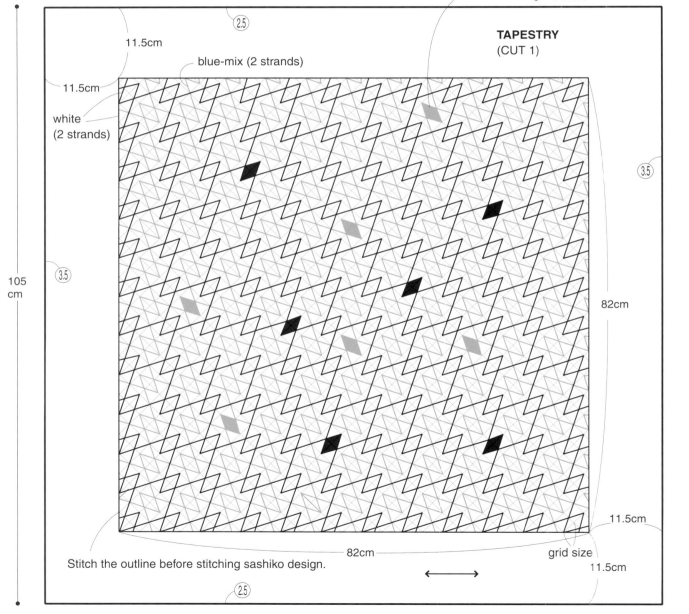

2.5

11.5cm

11.5cm

blue-mix (2 strands)

white (2 strands)

TAPESTRY
(CUT 1)

3.5

3.5

105 cm

82cm

82cm

11.5cm

11.5cm

grid size

Stitch the outline before stitching sashiko design.

2.5

105cm

Enlarge the grid to 2.5cm square.

#7 DOORWAY CURTAIN WITH "MOUNTAIN PASSES"

Life-Size Pattern on supplement (Side B)

Materials
110cm (43") x 140cm (55") cotton fabric
White sashiko thread
Finished Size: 71cm (28") W x 122cm (48") L

SEWING GUIDE

(Refer to supplementary pattern(side B), work sashiko
on two pieces of fabric, before making up.)

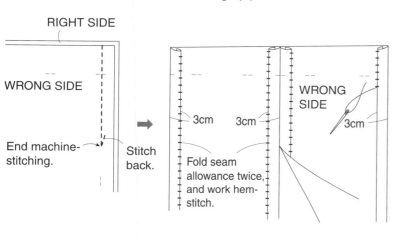

RIGHT SIDE

WRONG SIDE

End machine-stitching.

Stitch back.

3cm   3cm

Fold seam allowance twice, and work hem-stitch.

WRONG SIDE

3cm

CUTTING GUIDE

Cut out with added seam allowance of circled number width (cm).

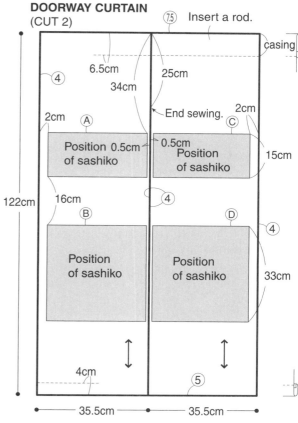

DOORWAY CURTAIN
(CUT 2)

⑦⑤ Insert a rod.

casing

6.5cm

④

34cm

25cm

End sewing.

2cm

2cm   Ⓐ   Position 0.5cm of sashiko   0.5cm Position of sashiko   Ⓒ

15cm

122cm

16cm   Ⓑ   ④   Ⓓ

Position of sashiko   Position of sashiko

33cm

④

4cm   ⑤

← 35.5cm →   ← 35.5cm →

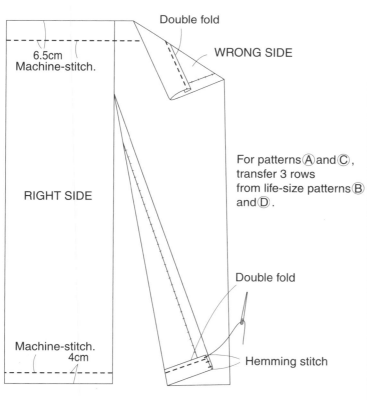

Double fold

WRONG SIDE

6.5cm
Machine-stitch.

RIGHT SIDE

For patterns Ⓐ and Ⓒ, transfer 3 rows from life-size patterns Ⓑ and Ⓓ.

Double fold

Hemming stitch

Machine-stitch.
4cm

COMPLETION

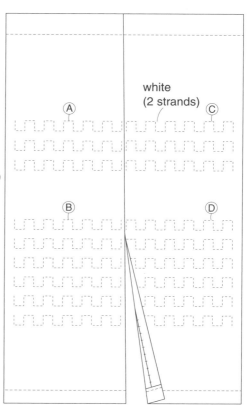

Ⓐ   white (2 strands)   Ⓒ

Ⓑ   Ⓓ

#2 DRAWSTRING BAG WITH "THUNDERBOLT" --- shown on page 30

Materials
30cm (12") x 60cm (24") indigo-dyed cotton fabric
40cm (16") x 50cm (20") cotton fabric for lining
150cm (59") 0.3cm-thick cord
Blue-mix sashiko thread

Finished Size:
21cm (8 1/4") W x 26cm (10 1/6") H

CUTTING GUIDE

Thread cord.
Thread cord.
Casing for cord
Ⓞ.5
CORD
Lining
LINING FABRIC

2.5cm
2cm
① 0.5cm

7cm
Outer
fabric
End
sewing.

Thread cord.
26cm
①
Position
of sashiko
18cm
OUTER
FABRIC
(CUT 1)
fold

24cm
4cm
②.5
13cm
1.5cm 5cm 5cm
POCKET
(CUT 1)
11cm
End
sewing.
0.2
cm
①
LINING
(CUT 1)
fold
①

4.5cm

26cm
Position
of sashiko
9cm
①

21cm

Cut out with added seam allowance of circled number width (cm).

End
sewing.
Thread cord.
2.5cm
7cm
②.5
Casing
for cord
Casing
for cord

21cm

Cut cord into halves (75cm each).

SEWING GUIDE

Stitch "THUNDERBOLT" referring to page 29, before making up.

1
2. Machine-stitch.
1, Double-fold.

1.5cm
POCKET
(WRONG SIDE)

POCKET
(WRONG
SIDE)

3. Fold in.

Attach pocket only on one side.

0.5cm

Openings
for cords

6cm

5cm

POCKET
(RIGHT
SIDE)
0.2cm

4. Machine-stitch.
LINING
(RIGHT SIDE)

2
Machine-stitch.
LINING
(RIGHT SIDE)
1cm

OUTER FABRIC
(WRONG SIDE)

Machine-
stitch.
1cm

3
Fold.

LINING
(WRONG SIDE)

2. Machine-
stitch.

1. Fold seam
allowance to
lining.

Stitch
back.
LINING
(RIGHT
SIDE)

5. Whipstitch.

OUTER FABRIC
(RIGHT SIDE)
End
sewing.
2cm

End sewing.

Leave openig
unsewn for
threading cord.

OUTER FABRIC
(WRONG SIDE)

3. Machine-stitch.
Fold.

Turn
over.

4. 2.5cm   Machine-stitch.

LINING
(RIGHT SIDE)

COMPLETION

Thread cords
and tie ends
into knots.

75cm-length
each

BACK

FRONT

74

#12 TABLE RUNNER WITH "FISHNET" --- shown on page 45

Life-Size Pattern on SUPPLEMENT (Side A)

CUTTING GUIDE

Add 1cm seam allowance all around.

Materials
110cm (44") x 60cm (24") cotton fabric
White sashiko thread
Finished Size: 27cm (10 1/2") W x 100cm (40") L

Refer to page 38 for stitching "FISHNET".

TABLE RUNNER
(CUT 1)

fold

27cm

100cm

SEWING GUIDE

(Stitch sashiko before making up.)

2. Machine-stitch.

WRONG SIDE

Leave 8-9cm
unsewn
for opening.

1. Fold.

Turn
over.

46cm   27cm

3. Whipstitch
to close
opening.

white(2 strands)

RIGHT SIDE

42.5cm   15cm

#13 FLOOR CUSHION COVERS WITH "SEVEN TREASURES" --- shown on page 46

CUTTING GUIDE

Life-Size Pattern on SUPPLEMENT (Side B)
Cut out with added seam allowance
of circled number width (cm).

Materials per piece
110cm (44") x 140cm (55")
 indigo-dyed cotton fabric
50cm (20") zip
Yellow green sashiko thread
Finished Size:
59cm (23 1/4") W x 63cm (25") L

4cm   (1)   4cm

(1.5)

1cm

Zip opening   Folding line   Folding line   Zip
                                                                    opening
         BACK   FRONT
                       (CUT 1)   BACK

(1.5)

4cm   (1)   4cm

59cm

51cm   63cm   12cm

COMPLETION

FRONT

59cm

63cm

1cm

Yellow green (2 strands)

Yellow green
(1 strand)

BACK

12cm

59cm

1cm

51cm

1cm

Stitch sashiko at
indicated areas,
referring to "SEVEN
TREASURES" on page 39.

Sew in the same manner
as cushion cover on page 70.

#9 THROW WITH "KEY PATTERN VARIATION"--- shown on page 36

Materials
38cm (15") x 640cm (7 yd.) cotton fabric
Blue-mix and blue-gradation sashiko threads
Finished Size: 138cm (54 1/2") W x 146cm (57 1/2") L

CUTTING GUIDE

Cut fabric into 4 strips with added seam allowance of circled number width (cm).

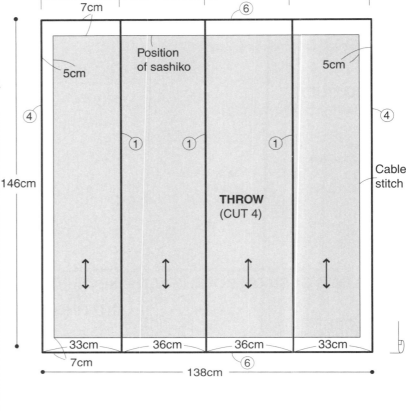

SEWING GUIDE

1

RIGHT SIDE

Join 4 strips in the same manner.

Machine-stitch.

WRONG SIDE

selvage

selvage

WRONG SIDE

Press seam open.

WRONG SIDE

WRONG SIDE

146cm

2 Stitch sashiko referring to the following page.
See page 12 for stitching "KEY PATTERN".

SHADING THE STAR

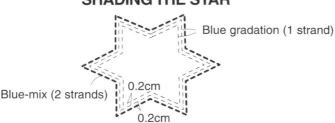

Blue gradation (1 strand)

Blue-mix (2 strands)

0.2cm

0.2cm

CABLE STITCH

Work a line of sashiko stitch,
and stitch back along it so that edges
of stitches overlap slightly.

3

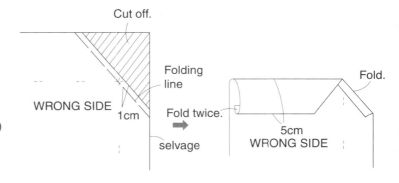

Cut off.

Folding line

WRONG SIDE

1cm

selvage

Fold twice.

Fold.

5cm

WRONG SIDE

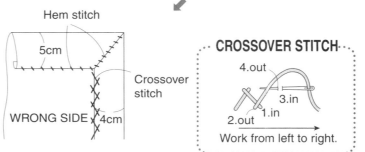

Hem stitch

5cm

Crossover stitch

WRONG SIDE 4cm

CROSSOVER STITCH

4.out

3.in

2.out

1.in

Work from left to right.

"KEY PATTERN" DESIGN LAYOUT

Life-size pattern is not provided. To make the shown size throw,
enlarge the design below until each triangular grid measures 2cm,
and transfer onto fabric.
Take 2 strands of blue-mix thread unless specified.
See previous page for shadowing the "stars".

Enlarge the grid size to 2cm.

33cm   36cm   36cm   33cm
Work cable stitches all around.

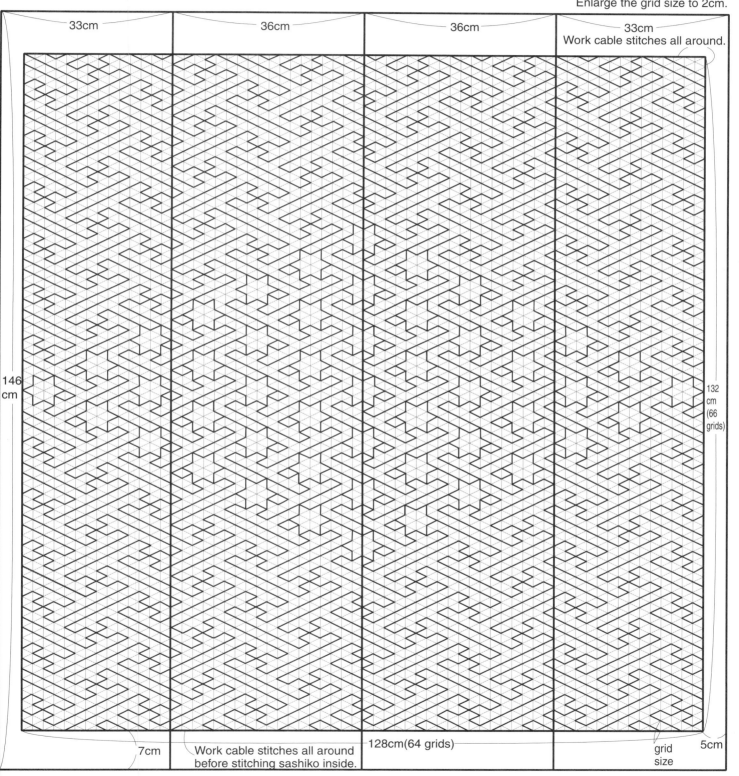

146 cm

132 cm (66 grids)

7cm   Work cable stitches all around
before stitching sashiko inside.   128cm(64 grids)   grid size   5cm

138cm

#10 KITCHEN TOWEL WITH "SEVEN TREASURES" --- shown on page 44
#11 KITCHEN TOWEL WITH "OCEAN WAVE" --- shown on page 44

Materials per piece
70cm (27 1/2") x 33cm (13") white cotton fabric
Sashiko threads (wine for #10, navy for #11)
Finished Size: 33cm (13") x 33cm (13")

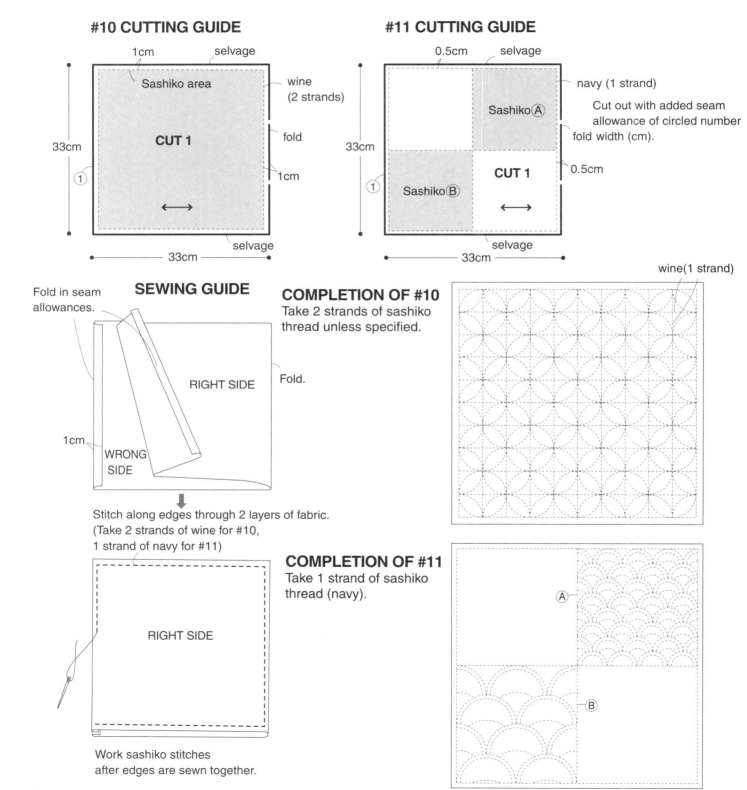

#10 CUTTING GUIDE

1cm
selvage
Sashiko area
wine
(2 strands)
fold
33cm
CUT 1
1cm
①
selvage
33cm

#11 CUTTING GUIDE

0.5cm
selvage
navy (1 strand)
Sashiko Ⓐ
Cut out with added seam
allowance of circled number
fold width (cm).
33cm
CUT 1
0.5cm
①
Sashiko Ⓑ
selvage
33cm

SEWING GUIDE

Fold in seam allowances.
RIGHT SIDE
Fold.
1cm
WRONG SIDE

Stitch along edges through 2 layers of fabric.
(Take 2 strands of wine for #10,
1 strand of navy for #11)

RIGHT SIDE

Work sashiko stitches
after edges are sewn together.

COMPLETION OF #10
Take 2 strands of sashiko
thread unless specified.

wine(1 strand)

COMPLETION OF #11
Take 1 strand of sashiko
thread (navy).

Ⓐ

Ⓑ

78

LIFE-SIZE PATTERN OF #10 (SEVEN TREASUERES)

Draw the whole design by shifting this pattern.
Take 2 strands of sashiko thread (wine) unless specified.

4

5

3

4

6

1

2

5

wine
(1 strand)

6

3

Position
of sashiko

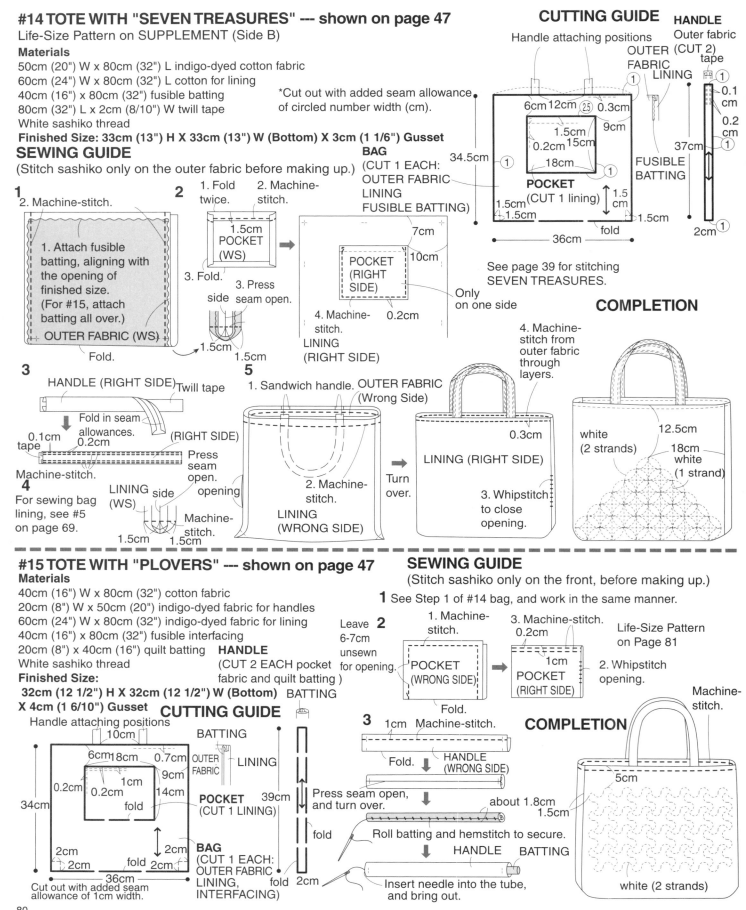

#14 TOTE WITH "SEVEN TREASURES" --- shown on page 47

Life-Size Pattern on SUPPLEMENT (Side B)

Materials
50cm (20") W x 80cm (32") L indigo-dyed cotton fabric
60cm (24") W x 80cm (32") L cotton for lining
40cm (16") x 80cm (32") fusible batting
80cm (32") L x 2cm (8/10") W twill tape
White sashiko thread

Finished Size: 33cm (13") H X 33cm (13") W (Bottom) X 3cm (1 1/6") Gusset

SEWING GUIDE
(Stitch sashiko only on the outer fabric before making up.)

CUTTING GUIDE

*Cut out with added seam allowance of circled number width (cm).

Handle attaching positions

HANDLE
Outer fabric (CUT 2)
tape
OUTER FABRIC
LINING
0.1 cm
0.2 cm
37cm
2cm

6cm 12cm ㉕ 0.3cm
9cm
34.5cm
1.5cm
0.2cm 15cm
18cm
POCKET (CUT 1 lining)
1.5 cm
1.5cm
1.5cm
fold
1.5cm
36cm

FUSIBLE BATTING

BAG
(CUT 1 EACH:
OUTER FABRIC
LINING
FUSIBLE BATTING)

See page 39 for stitching SEVEN TREASURES.

1
2. Machine-stitch.
1. Attach fusible batting, aligning with the opening of finished size.
(For #15, attach batting all over.)
OUTER FABRIC (WS)
Fold.

2
1. Fold twice.
2. Machine-stitch.
1.5cm
POCKET (WS)
3. Fold.
side
3. Press seam open.
1.5cm
1.5cm

7cm
10cm
POCKET (RIGHT SIDE)
0.2cm
Only on one side
4. Machine-stitch.
LINING (RIGHT SIDE)

3
HANDLE (RIGHT SIDE) Twill tape
Fold in seam allowances.
0.1cm tape
0.2cm
(RIGHT SIDE)
Press seam open.
Machine-stitch.

4
For sewing bag lining, see #5 on page 69.
LINING (WS)
side
opening
Machine-stitch.
1.5cm 1.5cm

5
1. Sandwich handle.
OUTER FABRIC (Wrong Side)
2. Machine-stitch.
LINING (WRONG SIDE)
Turn over.
0.3cm
LINING (RIGHT SIDE)
3. Whipstitch to close opening.

COMPLETION
4. Machine-stitch from outer fabric through layers.
white (2 strands)
12.5cm
18cm
white (1 strand)

#15 TOTE WITH "PLOVERS" --- shown on page 47

Materials
40cm (16") W x 80cm (32") cotton fabric
20cm (8") W x 50cm (20") indigo-dyed fabric for handles
60cm (24") W x 80cm (32") indigo-dyed fabric for lining
40cm (16") x 80cm (32") fusible interfacing
20cm (8") x 40cm (16") quilt batting
White sashiko thread

Finished Size:
32cm (12 1/2") H X 32cm (12 1/2") W (Bottom) X 4cm (1 6/10") Gusset

HANDLE
(CUT 2 EACH pocket fabric and quilt batting)
BATTING

CUTTING GUIDE

Handle attaching positions
10cm
6cm 18cm 0.7cm
OUTER FABRIC
LINING
9cm
1cm
0.2cm
0.2cm
14cm
34cm
fold
2cm
2cm
fold
2cm
2cm
36cm
Cut out with added seam allowance of 1cm width.

BATTING
POCKET (CUT 1 LINING)
39cm
fold
fold
2cm

BAG
(CUT 1 EACH:
OUTER FABRIC
LINING,
INTERFACING)

SEWING GUIDE
(Stitch sashiko only on the front, before making up.)

1 See Step 1 of #14 bag, and work in the same manner.

2
Leave 6-7cm unsewn for opening.
1. Machine-stitch.
POCKET (WRONG SIDE)
Fold.
3. Machine-stitch.
0.2cm
1cm
POCKET (RIGHT SIDE)
2. Whipstitch opening.

Life-Size Pattern on Page 81

3
1cm Machine-stitch.
Fold.
HANDLE (WRONG SIDE)
Press seam open, and turn over.
Roll batting and hemstitch to secure.
about 1.8cm
HANDLE
BATTING
Insert needle into the tube, and bring out.

COMPLETION
Machine-stitch.
5cm
1.5cm
white (2 strands)

LIFE-SIZE PATTERN OF #15 (PLOVERS)

Draw the whole design by shifting this pat.
Take 2 strands of sashiko thread (white).

6/#17 KITCHEN TOWELS WITH "PERSIMMON BLOSSOM" --- shown on page 53

Materials per piece
5cm x 35cm (13/4" x 13/4") white cotton fabric
.8cm (1/3") bias tape
Wine-colored sashiko thread
Finished Size: 34.5cm (13 6/10") W x 33cm (13") L

Life-Size Pattern of #16 on the following page 83
Life-Size Pattern of #17 on page 84

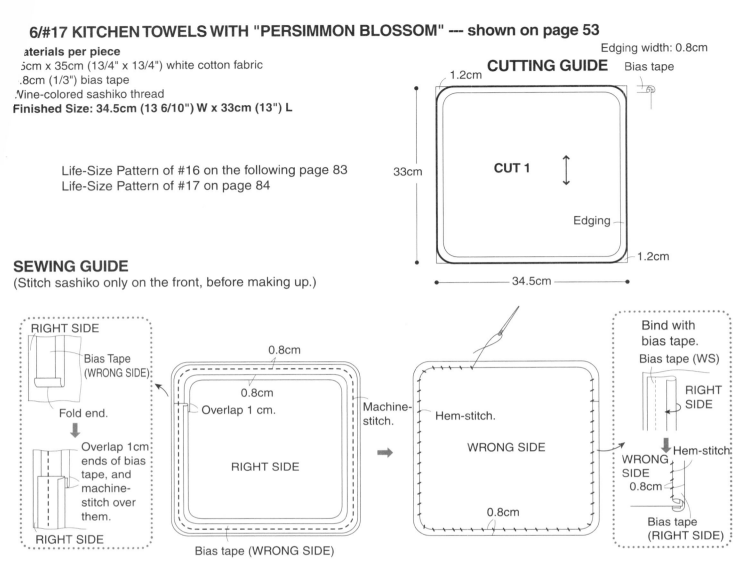

Edging width: 0.8cm

CUTTING GUIDE

Bias tape

1.2cm

33cm

CUT 1

Edging

1.2cm

34.5cm

SEWING GUIDE
(Stitch sashiko only on the front, before making up.)

RIGHT SIDE

Bias Tape (WRONG SIDE)

Fold end.

Overlap 1cm ends of bias tape, and machine-stitch over them.

RIGHT SIDE

0.8cm

0.8cm
Overlap 1 cm.

RIGHT SIDE

Bias tape (WRONG SIDE)

Machine-stitch.

Hem-stitch.

WRONG SIDE

0.8cm

Bind with bias tape.
Bias tape (WS)

RIGHT SIDE

Hem-stitch

WRONG SIDE

0.8cm

Bias tape (RIGHT SIDE)

COMPLETION OF #16
Take 2 strands of wine-color thread.

COMPLETION OF #17
Take 2 strands of wine-color thread.

LIFE-SIZE PATTERN OF #16 (PERSIMMON BLOSSOM)

Draw the whole design by shifting this pattern.
Take 2 strands of wine-color thread.

1

2

Binding

Pass thread on backside.

LIFE-SIZE PATTERN OF #17 (PERSIMMON BLOSSOM)

Draw the whole design by shifting this pattern.
Take 2 strands of wine-color thread.

Binding

84

Pass thread on backside.

#18 DRAWSTRING BAG WITH "FLORETS" --- shown on page 53

Materials
15cm (6") x 50cm (20") indigo-dyed cotton fabric
15cm (6") x 50cm (20") *tenugui* (Japanese washcloth) for lining
100cm (40") L x 0.2cm cord
Orange and white sashiko threads
Finished Size: 10cm (4") W x 23cm (9") L

Life-Size Pattern on SUPPLEMENT (Side B)

CUTTING GUIDE

Thread cord.

Outer fabric

Lining

cord

7cm   3cm   7cm

End sewing

23cm

1.5cm casing for cord

End sewing.

Position of sashiko

10cm

Fold

4cm

Cut cord in half (50cm).

Add 1cm seam allowance all around.

23cm

End sewing

casing for cord

1.5cm

End sewing.

CUT 1 EACH
Outer fabric
Lining

7cm   3cm   7cm

Thread cord.

•—10cm—•

SEWING GUIDE
(Stitch sashiko before making up.)

1

OUTER FABRIC
(WRONG SIDE)

Machine-stitch.

LINING (WRONG SIDE)

Machine-stitch.

2

Fold.

3. Machine-stitch.

Leave 8-9cm unsewn for opening.

End sewing.

LINING (WRONG SIDE)

Stitch back.

1. Press seam open.

End sewing.

2. Machine-stitch.

OUTER FABRIC (WS)

2. Machine-stitch.

Fold.

3

Layer outer fabric and lining and machine-stitch through.

Leave opening unsewn for threading cord.

Opening

Machine-stitch.

End sewing.

OUTER FABRIC (WS)

LINING (RIGHT SIDE)

LINING (WRONG SIDE)

OUTER FABRIC (RIGHT SIDE)

4

LINING (RIGHT SIDE)

Turn over the fabric using the opening. Whipstitch to close it.

5

2 pieces of 50cm-length cord

1. Machine-stitch.

1.5cm

OUTER FABRIC (RIGHT SIDE)

2. Thread cords and tie ends into knots.

COMPLETION

FRONT

BACK

orange (2 strands)

white (2 strands)

Work sashiko stitches as close to the edges as possible.

side

85

GRAPH PAPER
Adjust the size of grid or paper by photocopying in enlarged or reduced size.

DIAGONAL GRAPH PAPER
Adjust the size of grid or paper by photocopying in enlarged or reduced size.

INDEX

English Japanese Japanese Reading Page